THE CANADIAN THEATER, 1813

CASEMATE | ILLUSTRATED

THE CANADIAN THEATER, 1813

Richard V. Barbuto

CIS0052

Published in 2025 by
CASEMATE PUBLISHERS
1950 Lawrence Road, Havertown, PA 19083, USA
and
47 Church Street, Barnsley, S70 2AS, UK

Main text, Center of Military History, United States Army, Washington, D.C., 2013
Boxed text and timeline by Chris McNab © Casemate Publishers 2025

Paperback edition: ISBN 978-1-63624-542-3
Digital edition: ISBN 978-1-63624-543-0

A CIP record for this book is available from the British Library.

Maps by Myriam Bell
Design by Myriam Bell
Printed and bound in the United Kingdom by Short Run Press

For a complete list of Casemate titles, please contact:

CASEMATE PUBLISHERS (US)
Telephone (610) 853-9131
Fax (610) 853-9146
Email: casemate@casematepublishers.com
www.casematepublishers.com

CASEMATE PUBLISHERS (UK)
Telephone (0)1226 734350
Email: casemate@casemateuk.com
www.casemateuk.com

The Publisher's authorised representative in the EU for product safety is Authorised Rep Compliance Ltd., Ground Floor, 71 Lower Baggot Street, Dublin D02 P593, Ireland.
www.arccompliance.com

Contents

| Timeline

America had gone to war in June 1812 convinced that the conquest of Canada would be a simple matter. Such had not been the case. The nation's military had proven unprepared, its leaders often incompetent, and its men poorly trained and ill-equipped. Anglo-Canadian resistance had been stiffer than expected, while at home political and regional differences had hampered an effective mobilization of America's vastly superior resources. What successes the U.S. Army had achieved in 1812 had largely been overshadowed by ignominious defeats at Detroit, the River Raisin, and Queenston. By year's end, Canada stood defiant and America had actually lost some territory to Great Britain along the Northwest frontier.

1812
May 18 — Sir George Prévost, the Governor General of the Canadas, writes a letter to the Secretary of State for War and the Colonies and states that Fort George (present-day Niagara-on-the-Lake) was vulnerable to an American attack.

October — U.S. Department of the Navy appoints Capt. Isaac Chauncey to command in the Great Lakes, with orders to build ships and wrest control of the waters from the British Royal Navy.

1813
January 13 — President Madison appoints Brig. Gen. John Armstrong as the Secretary of War.

February 10 — U.S. commanders draw up a plan to attack Kingston then York from Sackett's Harbor, then move on to assault Fort George.

March — U.S. Brig. Gen. Zebulon M. Pike and his 15th Infantry advance from Plattsburgh to Sackett's Harbor on Lake Ontario.

▲ In Canada, Tecumseh's memory is respected for his fight against the American encroachment. This memorial marking the location of the battle of the Thames was photographed in the 1930s. (Archives of Ontario)

April 27	Battle of York. More than 2,700 U.S. troops storm Fort York (present-day Toronto) following an amphibious landing, defeating the British and Native American defenders and seizing the positions.
April 28–May 9	Siege of Fort Meigs. British and Native American forces place Fort Meigs, northwestern Ohio, under siege, but after bloody fighting fail to take the stronghold.
May 27	Some 4,000 U.S. troops make an amphibious assault on Fort George, led by Col. Winfield Scott. The Americans capture the fort, although most of the British garrison escape.
May 29	A British force commanded by Sir George Prevost assaults Sackett's Harbor, but the prepared American defenders repulse the attack.
June 1	Some 1,700 men under Gen. William Winder set out in pursuit of the British retreating from Fort George.
June 5	John Chandler's brigade joins Winder's force just west of Stoney Creek, near Lake Ontario.
June 6	Battle of Stoney Creek. Launching a night attack, British forces under Brig. Gen. John Vincent and Lt. Col. John Harvey secure a victory over the Americans, pushing them back toward the Niagara River.
June 24	Battle of Beaver Dams. An American column marching to destroy a British outpost at Beaver Dams is ambushed and defeated, with most of federal soldiers taken prisoner.
September 10	Battle of Lake Erie. A force of nine U.S. warships under the command of Oliver Hazard Perry defeats six Royal Navy vessels near Put-in-Bay, Ohio.
October 5	Battle of the Thames. Tecumseh's confederacy is defeated near Chatham, near Ontario, as the British retreat from Detroit. Tecumseh is killed.
October 26	Battle of the Chateauguay. An Anglo-Canadian and Native American force repel an American invasion of Lower Canada.
November 11	Battle of Crysler's Farm. An outnumbered Anglo-Canadian force defeats the rearguard of a U.S. campaign towards Montreal, leading to United States to abandon its St. Lawrence campaign.
December 19	The U.S.-held Fort Niagara is captured in a surprise British night assault.

| Introduction

Significant changes were going to be necessary if the United States was to achieve a more satisfactory outcome in the Canadian Theater in 1813. In the fall and winter of 1812/13, President James Madison's administration began to make some badly needed adjustments.

▼ This striking depicting of the battle of Queenston Heights, painted by the eyewitness artist James B. Dennis, shows American forces attempting to make an amphibious landing across the Niagara River on October 13, 1812. (NF Library)

Perhaps one of the greatest steps to improve the U.S. Army's performance was initiated by the U.S. Navy. Understanding that control of the Great Lakes would be essential to operations west of the St. Lawrence River, in October 1812 the Department of the Navy appointed Capt. Isaac Chauncey to command in the Great Lakes with orders to build ships and wrest control of the waters from the British Royal Navy. The department conferred upon Chauncey the courtesy title of

commodore given to officers who commanded squadrons. An able administrator, Chauncey energetically embarked on a naval arms race from his base at Sackett's Harbor, New York, on Lake Ontario.

In December 1812, President Madison relieved Secretary of War William Eustis. Eustis had been an adequate peacetime Secretary, but the requirements of the war had overwhelmed him. Madison directed that his Secretary of State, James Monroe, fill in as Secretary of War until he was able to find a permanent replacement. Monroe's tenure was brief, for in January 1813, the President appointed Brig. Gen. John Armstrong as the Secretary of War. Armstrong, a former senator and minister to France, had served in the Revolutionary War and had been present at British General John Burgoyne's surrender at Saratoga. He had also authored the notorious Newburgh Addresses that had nearly caused the Continental Army to mutiny in 1782. Armstrong commanded the defenses of New York City when he received the call to join the cabinet. The new Secretary had pretensions of being a strategist and an administrator, claims that his actions would tragically disprove.

Meanwhile, in January 1813, Congress bolstered the nation's military strength by adding nineteen infantry regiments and one regiment of rangers. President Madison filled the officer positions with persons nominated by congressmen and

▼ The imposing Fort Chambly was constructed during the 17th century as one of five bastions along the Richelieu River, a tributary of the St. Lawrence. During the War of 1812, the British used it as a military depot and barracks, with up to 6,000 troops stationed there. (Marc-Lautenbacher/CC BY-SA 4.0)

state governors. Although many of the new officers had held commissions in their states' militias, very few had seen active service. Since regimental commanders were responsible for filling the ranks of their companies, the Secretary of War assigned each regiment a geographic area from which to draw recruits. To facilitate recruiting, Congress had earlier raised the pay of all ranks. A private now earned $8 a month, a significant increase over the $5 monthly pay at the start of the war. Recruiting still lagged, however, so Congress authorized a third lieutenant and an additional sergeant for each company. This action gave regimental commanders more resources to direct their recruiting efforts. Unfortunately, the need for troops on the front lines was so demanding that companies were often marched off as soon as one hundred men could be recruited. Thus, a regiment rarely had all of its companies assembled together. A few companies might be actively serving on the frontier, while others were training elsewhere and yet others were still being recruited.

U.S. Army Rangers

Today, Ranger-qualified personnel are an elite stratum within the U.S. Army, one still imbued with the maverick mindset and unconventional doctrine of their historical forebears. The original Ranger concept was born in the 17th century. Small bands of hardy woodsmen, trappers and Indian fighters—self-sufficient types good with a musket, knife, and hatchet—were recruited in small numbers for military service in the American wilderness. Their training converted them into specialist light troops, ideally suited to scouting and raiding well away from the logistics and support of conventional forces. The first Ranger units were formed in the 1620s to fight Native Americans, but the formal establishment of the Rangers is closely identified with Colonel Benjamin Church's raising of a Ranger company during King Philip's War (1675–76). The most famous Ranger father figure, however, is Major Robert Rogers, who in 1755 established nine companies of "Roger's Rangers" to fight in the French and Indian War (1754–63). It was he who set down the 28 "Rules of Ranging" that are still followed to this day. The Rangers proved their worth as nimble, ruthless, and innovative warriors, and their ranks swelled to more than 1,200 men. The U.S. Congress recognized the value of such troops: in 1775 it authorized the establishment of eight companies of Rangers to fight the British, branded the Corps of Rangers in 1777. During the War of 1812, Ranger companies fought the British across territories from Ohio to Western Illinois.

More regiments meant more generals were required to lead them. President Madison named four new major generals: William Henry Harrison, James Wilkinson, Wade Hampton, and Morgan Lewis. Only Harrison would prove to be a successful commander. Madison also appointed seven new brigadier generals. Finally, Armstrong and Madison rationalized command issues by creating nine military districts and appointing generals to direct each. Assisted by a complete staff, each general would command all regular troops and militia in federal service within the boundaries of his district.

As the nation attempted to improve its military organization and leadership, Secretary Armstrong sent to the Army's senior officer, Maj. Gen. Henry Dearborn, a strategy for 1813 that designated control of Lake Ontario as the key to future operations against Lower Canada. The Secretary directed General Dearborn to send four thousand troops to the naval base at Sackett's Harbor and three thousand to Buffalo, New York. Cooperating with Captain Chauncey, Dearborn would first attack the British naval base at Kingston and then follow with attacks on York and the British forts along the Niagara in Upper Canada. Destruction of the British squadron at Kingston would give control of Lake Ontario to Chauncey. Dearborn and Chauncey, vastly overestimating British troop strength at Kingston, believed that city to be too strong to attack. They offered Armstrong a counterproposal to first raid York to capture or destroy vessels being built there. Then, they would attack Fort George at the northern mouth of the Niagara River. Once solidly positioned at Fort George, Dearborn could handily cut the British line of communications westward. The British presence on the Upper Great Lakes would wither and disappear. Reluctantly, Armstrong agreed to this new strategy. Madison and his cabinet needed a victory to dispel the gloom of the failed campaigns of 1812.

Meanwhile, Lt. Gen. Sir George Prevost, Governor General of British North America, was astounded that the Canadian provinces had survived the 1812 campaign. Prevost understood that resources from Great Britain would continue

▲ *James Madison, engraving by David Edwin. (New York Public Library)*

to be meager as long as the empire was locked in a life or death struggle with Napoleonic France. The government in London considered the war with America a sideshow to the main event in Europe. Cautious by nature, Prevost wisely set forth a defensive strategy along the border with the United States. In his judgment, the cities of Montreal and Quebec were essential to maintaining a British presence in North America. If necessary, territory in the province of Upper Canada could be lost temporarily. As long as the British held Quebec and Montreal, British forces could eventually recapture any lost lands to the west. He therefore issued orders to his subordinate generals not to take undue risks and to maintain their fighting strength as much as possible. Thus, the year 1813 began with the British on the defensive and the Americans anxious to advance deep into Canada in order to achieve their war aims.

▲ *John Armstrong*, by John Wesley Jarvis. (National Portrait Gallery, Smithsonian)

▲ Map 1

Zebulon Pike (1779–1813)

Born on January 5, 1779, in Lamington, New Jersey, Zebulon Pike pursued a military career from 1799, when he was commissioned as a second lieutenant in the U.S. Army. Prior to the War of 1812, Pike made a prominent name for himself as a military explorer. He was ideal for such a role—observant, diplomatic, hardy, and resourceful. In 1805, General in Chief James Wilkinson ordered now Lieutenant Pike to explore the American Northeast, specifically to find the headwaters of the Mississippi, establish U.S. legal rights over discovered territories, and negotiate with Native American tribes. His epic 2,000-mile journey was followed by another major expedition in 1807, this time to the territories around the Arkansas and Red Rivers in the Southwest; his subsequent report on Spanish Santa Fe helped to fuel the U.S. drive to expand into Texas.

Pike's expeditions became famous for their endurance and danger, as much as their cultural, geographical, and natural insights. In 1811, however, he returned to orthodox military service, fighting with the 4th Infantry Regiment at the battle of Tippecanoe against Tecumseh.

▲ *Zebulon Pike*, from a print dated 1814. (Library of Congress)

Shortly after the outbreak of the War of 1812, Pike was promoted to colonel of the 15th Infantry Regiment. He was subsequently killed leading a campaign into Canada, when the British blew up the powder magazine at Fort York on April 27, 1813.

Operations

Once Madison and his cabinet agreed on York as an appropriate first objective, Dearborn and Chauncey began planning in earnest. Chauncey believed that the British were building two brigs of eighteen guns each at York. He also surmised that York had immense amounts of naval stores to support the Royal Navy on Lake Ontario. Chauncey expected that a raid on York would decisively shift the balance of naval power to the Americans. The two commanders agreed that they would follow up the raid on York with an attack on Fort George. Simultaneously, American forces at Buffalo would cross the Niagara River to seize Fort Erie at the southern entrance to the river. With Fort Erie in American hands, the various American war vessels hemmed in at the naval yard at nearby Black Rock, New York, could escape into Lake Erie to augment the squadron being built at Erie, Pennsylvania. Chauncey sent Master Commandant Oliver Hazard Perry to Erie to supervise shipbuilding so as to gain control of Lake Erie in the summer. Control of Lake Erie would enable General Harrison's Northwestern Army to recover Detroit and to clear the British from western Upper Canada (Map 1).

Dearborn chose newly promoted Brig. Gen. Zebulon M. Pike to lead the assault on York. Already famous as a western explorer, Pike had also earned a reputation as a gentleman and a competent commander who led by example. As a colonel, Pike had commanded the 15th U.S. Infantry, a regiment raised largely in New Jersey. He had trained his soldiers and had ensured that they were well cared for during the harsh winter of 1812/13. In March, Pike and his 15th Infantry trekked

◄▲ An august full-length portrait of Sir George Prevost by Robert Field. Prevost had a long and stirring military career, topped by his role as Commander in Chief of British land forces during the War of 1812. (The Halifax Club)

◄ A fitting memorial to Zebulon Pike, and his fellow officers, consisting of a block of stone surmounted by a short-barreled mortar. The grave marker is located in the Military Cemetery within the Sackets Harbor Battlefield State Historic Site. (LOC)

through deep snow from Plattsburgh to Sackett's Harbor. Following promotion to brigadier general in April, Pike assumed command of Dearborn's 1st U.S. Brigade.

One of Pike's key subordinates, Bvt. Lt. Col. Benjamin Forsyth, shared few similarities with his commander. Colonel Forsyth commanded a battalion of the U.S. Rifle Regiment. While brave like Pike, Forsyth was neither a stickler for discipline nor as industrious. Pike trained and inspected and otherwise kept his men engaged in soldiering when not in action. Forsyth allowed his riflemen much freedom when not in action, but in combat they could be counted on to press the fight to the utmost. However, he turned a blind eye to his men's looting of the dead, wounded, and captured enemy. Pike and Forsyth played conspicuous roles in the raid on York.

The Raid on York, April 1813

Shortly after the ice had receded from Sackett's Harbor, Chauncey ordered the embarkation of the landing force. Starting on April 20, eighteen hundred soldiers and eight hundred sailors crowded aboard thirteen warships.

▼ The British sloop-of-war *Sir Isaac Brock* under construction at York, Upper Canada, in 1812–13. The unlaunched ship was set on fire on its stocks by its owners to prevent its falling into the hands of the Americans in April 1813. (Toronto Public Library)

Embarkation took three long days, and the squadron had barely cleared the harbor when a heavy rainstorm drenched sailors and soldiers alike. Only half of the passengers could fit in the comparative shelter below deck. Those remaining were forced to withstand strong wind and driving rain on the overcrowded decks. Unable to move through the heavy storm, Commodore Chauncey ordered the

squadron returned to calmer waters. Chauncey started again on April 25; however, strong waves jostled the vessels and many soldiers were seasick for much of the voyage. Finally, the next evening, the Americans came into sight of their objective, the village and naval base at York.

British Maj. Gen. Roger Hale Sheaffe defended York with about 400 regulars, 525 militia and shipwrights, and as many as 100 native warriors. The main defenses of York were west of the town and boatyard. These defenses consisted of the garrison—a group of barracks surrounded by an earthen rampart and a number of cannon—and three other batteries extending westward: Government House Battery, Half Moon Battery, and Western Battery. To the west of Western Battery, the land was flat and heavily wooded, except for a cleared area around a ruined French fortification, Fort Rouillé. Chauncey anchored his squadron in an extended line opposite Fort Rouillé, well out of range of the British batteries. At 0700, he ordered the troops to disembark.

Chauncey had enough ships' boats to carry three hundred men to shore at a time. Forsyth took one hundred seventy of his men on the first wave, alongside soldiers of the 15th Infantry. Indian warriors waiting on shore opened fire, which the riflemen returned from their landing boats. Forsyth's riflemen hit the shore, scrambled over the bank, spread out, and began a relentless movement through the woods, inflicting casualties among the native warriors. East of the riflemen, boatloads of the 15th Infantry landed, formed into platoons, and climbed the banks. There they were met by the concentrated musketry of the grenadier company of the 8th Regiment of Foot. The grenadiers followed up their gunfire with a bayonet assault that forced the American infantry back down the embankment. However, the American riflemen salvaged the situation. Forsyth was everywhere encouraging and guiding his men. The riflemen's fire drove off the Indian warriors, and the British grenadiers, cut to pieces, withdrew as well.

General Pike and his staff landed with the next wave of attackers, as General Dearborn watched the assault from his flagship. Pike formed his infantry in line facing east with Forsyth's riflemen on the left. With regimental flags flying, the Americans entered the clearing around Fort Rouillé. General Sheaffe, at the head of a mixed force of regulars and militia, entered the clearing from the east. The guns of the American schooners opened fire on the British with grapeshot.

American musket, rifle, and cannon fire proved too intense for the defenders. After several minutes, Sheaffe ordered his troops to withdraw eastward toward the Western Battery. The British commander realized that these Americans were not like the amateurs he had easily beaten six months earlier at Queenston Heights.

Over the next two hours, boats shuttled between ship and shore bringing more Americans to the fight. Elements of the 6th, 15th, and 16th U.S. Infantry as well as two volunteer companies, the Albany Greens and the Baltimore Volunteers, came ashore. West Point graduate Lt. Alexander C. W. Fanning of the 3d U.S. Artillery and his gunners manhandled a 6-pounder gun and a howitzer out of the boats and up the embankment. With no horses, the artillerymen pulled guns and limbers along a path through the woods. Pike formed his brigade in column and readied it to move eastward through the woods and against the British defenses. American schooners moved opposite the four British batteries and opened up a heavy fire. Then, disaster befell the British. A gunner in Western Battery accidentally brought his lit portfire into contact with a box of artillery ammunition. The resulting explosion killed about a dozen artillerists and wounded many more. The British regulars recovered quickly, but many Canadian militiamen drifted away from the danger.

General Sheaffe, seeing the strong American brigade approaching the Western Battery, gave orders to abandon

▼ 1st U.S. Rifle Regiment, by Don Troiani. (Don Troiani Image Bank)

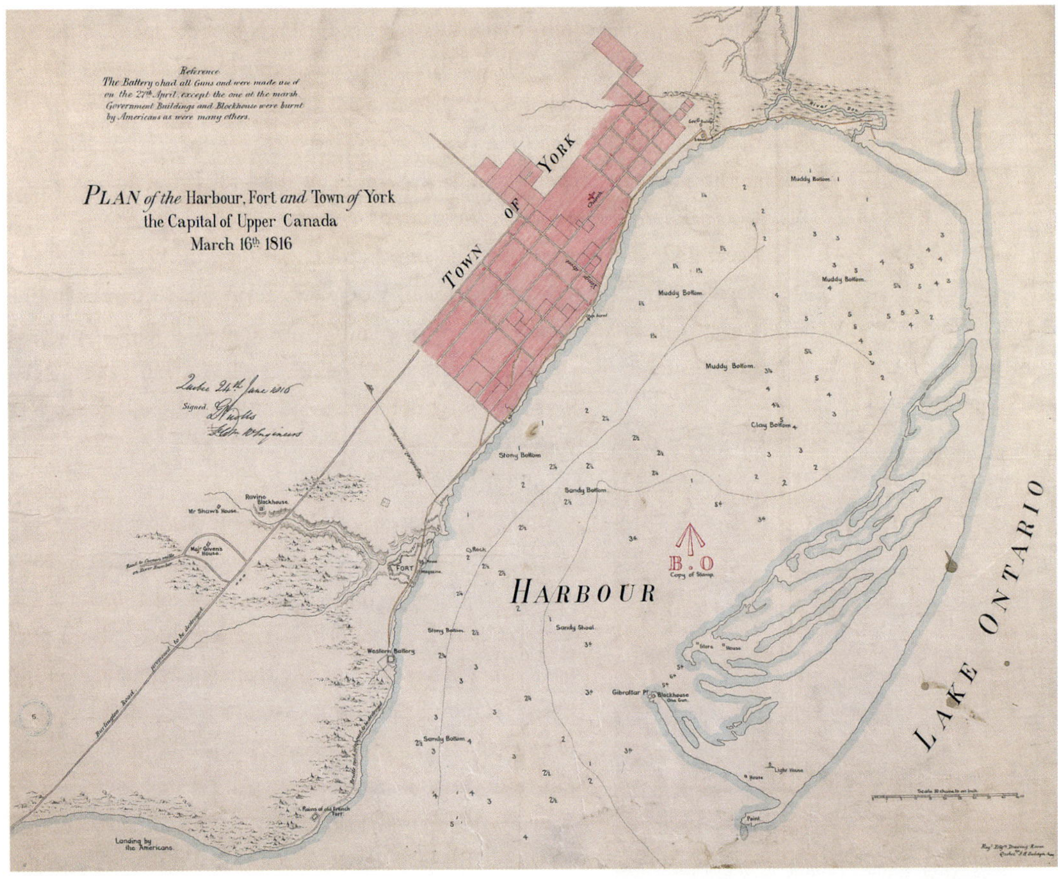

that position and the Half Moon Battery to its rear. He apparently had decided that he could not successfully defend York with the meager force at his disposal and began extracting his regulars from the town. General Pike sent his advance guard, four companies of the 6th U.S. Infantry, ahead. They discovered that the British appeared to be gathering at Government House Battery. Pike ordered his artillery to send some rounds into the British defenses.

A little after 1300 catastrophe struck. A massive explosion erupted from the earth near the Government House Battery. Three hundred barrels of gunpowder ignited and instantaneously pulverized the roof and walls of the stone magazine in which they had been stored. A fireball rose, followed by a high column of black smoke. Timber, stone, and iron cannon shot were thrown high into the air before raining down on British and American alike up to five hundred yards from the explosion. Col. Cromwell Pearce, the commander of the 16th U.S. Infantry, recorded that "the noise of the explosion was tremendous. The earth shook and the sun was darkened, while the crashing of the rocks, high in the air, and the groans of the wounded, rendered it one of the most awful sights in nature." American losses were 39 killed

▲ A plan of the harbor, fort, and town of York, as seen one year after the end of the War of 1812. The location of the fort is marked just southwest of the town, overlooking the harbor. (Toronto Public Library)

and 224 wounded in the explosion. The wounded suffered cruelly: limbs and skulls fractured and flesh pierced by shards of iron and splinters of timber. General Pike was among the wounded, tragically hit by a large stone that crushed his spine. His staff evacuated him to the fleet.

What happened next reflects immense credit on the American soldier. In the face of extraordinary casualties, those still remaining on their feet did not falter. The officers rallied their men and the advance continued, around the blackened crater where the ammunition magazine had been minutes earlier, and through the abandoned garrison. Moments later, Colonel Pearce came upon a group of Canadian militia officers carrying a white flag. Before he left York with his regulars, General Sheaffe had ordered these incredulous militia officers to surrender their village. They could not believe that Sheaffe had abandoned the provincial capital without a more determined fight.

Lt. Col. George Mitchell of the 3d U.S. Artillery negotiated a simple surrender document that respected private property, but yielded public property to the victors. The Americans occupied the village, although not until the British had managed to burn a ship that was under construction. Pike died aboard the schooner *Madison*, Chauncey's flagship. His friends placed a captured flag under his head before he expired. Americans, British, and Canadians alike turned their attention to treating the hundreds of wounded. A handful of American regimental surgeons and surgeon's mates worked through the next two days with little sleep or food. William Beaumont, surgeon's mate of the 6th U.S. Infantry, recalled that his fellow surgeons were "wading in blood, cutting off arms, legs, and trepanning heads to rescue their fellow creatures from untimely death."

Neither Dearborn and Chauncey nor their officers were able to maintain control of all of their soldiers and seamen. Some Americans slipped away from their units to pillage local homes. Unknown arsonists burned some public buildings, including the parliament buildings of Upper Canada. While many vandals were clearly American military men, a few were Canadian civilians. When the Americans had arrived in the village of York, they had freed a number of inmates from the local jail. These prisoners were disaffected Canadians, many of whom had been born in the United States and had spoken against the war or had evaded duty in the militia. These individuals also contributed to the mischief. Eventually, Dearborn put enough patrols on the streets to stop the looting, but much damage had already occurred.

For three days after the raid, soldiers and sailors loaded a mountain of captured supplies and equipment aboard Chauncey's ships. Immense quantities of food, sails, cables, iron implements, tools, and artillery came into the possession of the attackers. The Americans then loaded the wounded below deck, and finally, the rest of the soldiers came aboard. Soldiers and sailors crammed the decks, with no space below. Heavy winds blew adversely into York Harbor for days, thus preventing the

Profile:
Commodore Isaac Chauncey (1772–1840)

Born on February 20, 1772, in Black Rock, Connecticut, Isaac Chauncey would dedicate his life in the service to and improvement of the early U.S. Navy. He entered the merchant marine in his late teens, evident competence bringing his first command at the age of just 19. In 1798 he transferred to the U.S. Navy, commissioned as a young lieutenant. International circumstances meant that he gained operational and leadership experience rapidly, particularly during the Quasi-War with France in 1798–1800 and as a frigate commander in the Mediterranean during the First Barbary War (1801–05). Promoted to captain in 1806, Chauncey showed that he could also handle major on-shore naval management roles; he was appointed the commandant of the U.S. Navy Yard at Brooklyn, New York, a position he held until 1813.

In the War of 1812, Chauncey was deployed to the Great Lakes region, where he directed the construction of an inland U.S. fleet on Lake Ontario as a counterweight to the Royal Navy. He also led or participated in numerous raids and fleet actions around the lake, including against York and Burlington Heights. His career tempo remained brisk even after the end of the war. He was appointed leader of Portsmouth Navy Yard, at Kittery, Maine, and again of Brooklyn Navy Yard between 1824 and 1833. He commanded the Mediterranean Squadron in 1816–1818 and rose to the President of the Board of Navy Commissioners by 1837. This latter service took him up to his death on January 27, 1840.

▲ A portrait of Commodore Isaac Chauncey in his full dress uniform. Given his lifetime's service to the U.S. Navy, there is scarce any other clothing that would adequately represent him. (Smithsonian American Art Museum, Bequest of Mary Elizabeth Spencer)

ships from making headway out into the lake while cold rain drenched those on deck. Dysentery broke out and all suffered enormously. Finally, twelve days after landing at York, the squadron made its way across the lake and dropped anchor at the mouth of Four Mile Creek, New York, named for its distance from Fort Niagara. The troops came ashore, but no tents awaited them. The men had to bed down on wet ground and were caught in frequent rainstorms. The American landing force of eighteen hundred had suffered about three hundred twenty casualties, mostly to the magazine explosion. This reflected a casualty rate of nearly 18 percent, a heavy loss.

General Pike's death proved particularly tragic. Surgeon's mate William Beaumont wrote to his parents of the "death of our ablest, bravest & highly respected, & almost adored Col. Pike, in consequence of the explosion. His cool, calm, intrepid & brave conduct, during the engagement, unites the highest esteem & admiration of all Officers of the Army & cannot but remain the tribute of universal applause & approbation!" Despite the losses sustained in the battle and sickness among the survivors, Dearborn and Chauncey immediately began preparations to capture Fort George and to seize the Niagara Peninsula.

▶ *United States Infantry Pvt. 15th Regiment, 1812–1813*, by Don Troiani. (Don Troiani Image Bank)

Operations on the Niagara Peninsula, May–June 1813

The raid on York represented a well-executed joint operation between the U.S. Army and Navy. The subsequent landing at Fort George, a much larger operation, was also planned and executed to near perfection. Chauncey's fleet shuttled several thousand soldiers from Sackett's Harbor until Dearborn had about forty-seven hundred regulars at Four Mile Creek. Dearborn organized his force into an advance guard and three brigades.

General Dearborn gave command of the advance guard to Col. Winfield Scott. Scott had commanded American forces atop Queenston Heights in the last phase of that battle. Captured and eventually exchanged, Scott had been promoted and given command of the 2d U.S. Artillery. Dearborn held Scott in high regard and had made him his adjutant general. For the Fort George operation, Scott handpicked his landing force. It included Forsyth's rifle battalion, three infantry companies, and two artillery companies fighting as infantry.

Dearborn's brigade commanders represented a mixed bag. Brig. Gen. John Boyd commanded the 1st U.S. Brigade. Boyd had spent nine years in India commanding native forces, and returned to America in 1798 a rich man. He had commanded the 4th U.S. Infantry at the battle of Tippecanoe in 1811 and was promoted to brigadier general soon after the declaration of war. Brig. Gen. William Winder commanded the 2d U.S. Brigade in Dearborn's army. A prominent Baltimore lawyer and militia officer who lacked military experience, Winder had risen rapidly over a year's time to the rank of brigadier general. Some considered Winder's promotion politically motivated because he was the nephew of the Federalist Governor of Maryland. Brig. Gen. John Chandler commanded the 3d U.S. Brigade. A veteran of the

Profile:
General Henry Dearborn (1751–1829)

Henry Dearborn was a man whose reputation was both made and weakened by war. He was born on February 23, 1751, into a distinguished New Hampshire family. He was laying the foundations of a promising career in medicine when the Revolutionary War broke out in 1775. A true patriot, he formed his own militia and joined the Continental Army, leading troops in many major engagements, including at Bunker Hill, Quebec (where he was captured, but later exchanged), Saratoga, Monmouth, and Yorktown. He also took a leadership role in the expedition against the Iroquois Confederacy in 1779. By war's end he was a colonel in rank, rising to major general by 1789. At this point he retired from military service to pursue a career in politics, becoming U.S. Representative for Massachusetts (1793–97) and Secretary of War (1801–09) under the administration of President Thomas Jefferson; in the latter capacity, he ordered construction of a fort on western Lake Michigan, the seed of the city of Chicago.

During the War of 1812, Dearborn was called back into the ranks of the U.S. Army by President James Madison. His campaigns in Canada, however, were characterized by defeat and poor leadership, thus he was relieved of his command on July 6, 1813. Thereafter, he struggled to maintain his reputation. His attempt to become Governor of Massachusetts failed, and his last official government position was as Minister to Portugal (1822–24). Dearborn retired in 1824 and died in Roxbury, Massachusetts, on June 6, 1829.

Revolutionary War from Massachusetts, Chandler had been a blacksmith, tavern keeper, militia officer, and state senator.

A political appointee, Chandler received a commission as a brigadier general in 1812 and, like Winder, had seen no military action thus far in the war.

Too ill to command on the ground himself, Dearborn gave command of the operation to his second in command, Maj. Gen. Morgan Lewis, who also lacked recent military experience. Another veteran of the Revolutionary War and a former governor of New York, Lewis was the brother-in-law of the Secretary of War and a personal friend of the President.

Fort George was located near the northern mouth of the Niagara River, about one thousand yards directly south of Fort Niagara on the opposite shore. The small village of Newark (now called Niagara-on-the-Lake) was immediately northwest of Fort George and across the river from Fort Niagara. Fort George consisted of six bastions connected by an earthen parapet topped by a wooden palisade. A shallow ditch surrounded the fortification. Inside were a few wooden barracks, warehouses, and blockhouses as well as a stone magazine. The British commander, Maj. Gen. John Vincent, defended Fort George with five artillery pieces: three guns and two mortars. He had eleven other pieces located in five detached batteries along the riverbank facing Fort Niagara. The Americans had twenty-five artillery pieces mounted in Fort Niagara or in batteries along the eastern riverbank.

General Vincent had a slender force under his command—one thousand regulars, three hundred militia, and sixty native warriors. He was well aware that

▼ Today Fort George National Historic Site, Niagara-on-the-Lake, is a popular tourist attraction featuring restored buildings, musketry demonstrations, guided tours, and military music from the 41st Fife and Drum Corps. (Ken Smith/ CC BY-SA 3.0)

▲ *Winfield Scott,* by Joseph Wood. (Library of Congress)

his fort was a major American objective. He did not know, however, how the Americans would attack. Therefore, he split his meager command into three elements. He placed one force along a likely landing beach on Lake Ontario to the west of Niagara. He sent another to guard against a potential river crossing south of the fort. He retained the last element under his personal command at Fort George. Vincent had troops and guns thinly spread along a five-mile arc. While he fully intended to defend the fort, he also understood that his ultimate goal was to keep his forces intact for future operations.

General Dearborn gave Colonel Scott the task of planning the attack on Fort George. Scott aimed to destroy Vincent's division, not just seize the fortification. There were two escape routes out of Fort George. One route headed west along the shore of Lake Ontario. This would take Vincent's retreating army to Burlington Heights, a natural defensive position overlooking Burlington Bay at the head of Lake Ontario. The second route that Vincent might take was the river road connecting Fort George with the village of Queenston and

▶ A plaque, cannon, and stone marker at Burlington Heights indicate the place where (as declared on the plaque) "in June, 1813, General John Vincent made the successful night attack on the invaders at Stoney Creek" and from where "in December, 1813, the force which retook Fort George and carried Fort Niagara by assault, began its march." (Laslovarga/CC BY-SA 3.0)

the security of Queenston Heights. Scott planned to close both escape routes. The major landing would take place west of Niagara between that town and Two Mile Creek. The bulk of the American army would land there and head directly toward Fort George. However, Scott planned for Col. James Burn and his 2d Regiment of Light Dragoons to cross the Niagara River several miles south of Fort George and block the road leading to Queenston.

Scott and Chauncey then focused on the Navy's role. In this, they were assisted by Master Commandant Perry. When the energetic Perry had learned of the planned attack, he had rushed to Fort Niagara to be a part of the upcoming battle. The day before the landing, Chauncey and Perry reconnoitered the shore from the schooner *Lady of the Lake*. They planted buoys marking the location for each of Chauncey's vessels so that they would be well positioned to cover the landing with naval gunfire. After midnight on May 27, thousands of American soldiers at Four Mile Creek east of Fort Niagara entered bateaux and scows. Chauncey's vessels pulled the landing craft out into Lake Ontario about two miles from shore.

Fort George

Construction of Fort George on the western banks of the Niagara River began in the 1790s. It was intended as a replacement for Fort Niagara on the opposite bank; this fort had been ceded to the United States as part of the Treaty of Paris. The first iteration of the fort in 1796 consisted of a combined blockhouse/barracks, a gunpowder magazine, and two warehouses. By 1802, however, it had been substantially developed, with six earth-and-log bastions connected by a wooden palisade and numerous other buildings, including blockhouses, kitchens, separate barracks, a hospital, and an officers' quarters. A sentinel over the river, Fort Niagara became the British Army headquarters in the theater and a major depot of the Indian Department.

During the War of 1812, Fort George was the HQ of the British Centre Division. As this book relates, the fort was heavily embattled during the conflict, changing hands twice and being smashed by artillery fire. The war ended with the fort in British possession. Some rebuilding work was undertaken, but during the 1820s the fort sank into neglect, disuse, and ruin. From the 1860s, now under Canadian ownership, it was transferred into private hands, but on May 21, 1921, the site was named as a National Historic Site of Canada, a stone cairn marking its location. Today, Fort George is an active and well-preserved historical museum site.

THE BATTLE OF FORT GEORGE
LA BATAILLE DE FORT GEORGE

On 25 May, 1813, the American fleet and the batteries at Fort Niagara across the river began a devastating two-day bombardment of Fort George. On the 27th a large American force was landed and after a brief engagement in which his outnumbered garrison sustained heavy casualties, Brigadier-General John Vincent made an orderly withdrawal towards Burlington. The capture of Fort George left the Americans in control of the Niagara frontier, but Vincent's troops a week later won a decisive victory at Stoney Creek, preventing the Americans from gaining the whole peninsula.

Le 25 mai 1813, la flotte américaine et les batteries du fort Niagara, commencèrent à bombarder le fort George. Le 27, de nombreuses troupes américaines débarquèrent. Après un bref engagement, au cours duquel sa garnison, bien inférieure en nombre, subit de lourdes pertes, le brigadier-général John Vincent se replia sur Burlington. La capture du fort laissait les Américains maîtres de la région frontalière du Niagara. Une semaine plus tard, les troupes de Vincent remportèrent une victoire décisive à Stoney Creek, empêchant ainsi les Américains de prendre possession de toute la péninsule.

Historic Sites and Monuments Board of Canada.
Commission des lieux et monuments historiques du Canada.

Government of Canada · 1923 · Gouvernement du Canada

Each brigade formed in a line of boats with Scott's eight hundred men in twenty vessels in the lead. When dawn came, a heavy fog covered the lake. Soldiers and sailors waited impatiently to begin their rush to the shore. When the fog eventually cleared, General Vincent saw sixteen ships and a vast number of bateaux laden with soldiers moving, relentlessly, toward the landing beach. Moments later, more than fifty guns from the American squadron roared out. Solid shot and exploding shells crashed onto the shore and the fields beyond. Perry moved between ships in a gig and shouted commands to the ships' captains to better adjust their gunfire. British infantry and native warriors kept under the cover of streambeds as Scott and his advance guard approached.

Despite the heavy naval gunfire, the British and natives fired at Scott's men as they landed. The American advance guard formed under fire and assaulted up the twelve-foot-high embankment just beyond the landing. Fighting was desperate. Scott nearly reached the top of the bank when he dodged a bayonet thrust, lost his footing, and fell back down onto the beach. Dearborn, watching from the flagship

Spiking the guns

By the 19th century, artillery was the primary killer on the battlefield. Overrunning enemy artillery batteries, therefore, was a prized goal for infantry and cavalry, not only for relieving the volumes of incoming shot, but also to capture and repurpose valuable guns. But on an undecided battlefield, the enemy might recapture both positions and weapons. Seen from the other side, an artillery battery might be compelled to abandon its position and its inconveniently heavy weapons, and therefore needed to prevent the guns from being turned around and used to engage their former owners. A cannon could be rendered temporarily unusable by a variety of means, but one of the more decisive was "spiking." To spike a gun, the soldier hammered an iron spike down into the cannon's touch-hole, then snapped off any exposed head. (The touch-hole was the open passage connecting the ignition mechanism with the main charge in the chamber.) For good measure, the soldier might also run a rammer down the barrel to bend the tip of the spike inside the bore. The spike itself could be a purpose-designed barbed spike or, if not available, a common nail. If need be, even the tip of a bayonet or a rat-tipped file could be used. Once spiked, the touch-hole would need to be redrilled to get the cannon working again—lengthy engineering work not possible in the fury of the battle.

Madison, cried out that Scott had been killed. Winfield Scott picked himself up and climbed back up the bank.

General Boyd's brigade landed, formed, and threw its weight into the assault. Eventually the Americans gained the crest of the embankment. The British were hardly twenty yards away when the two sides opened up a furious, violent firefight. Despite the arrival of reinforcements, the British could not stand up to superior numbers. Vincent, well aware that he was vastly outnumbered, ordered his men to abandon Fort George and to move on the southerly road toward Queenston. Along the way, he picked up another road leading westward to Burlington Heights and relative safety. He ordered the guns of Fort George spiked and the magazine and bastions blown up.

With the British retreating, Scott formed his advance guard to maintain contact. Forsyth's riflemen, advancing in a skirmish line, followed the enemy. Scott himself took two companies of artillery and moved directly to Fort George. He found a horse and galloped toward the fort ahead of his men. Just as he approached the

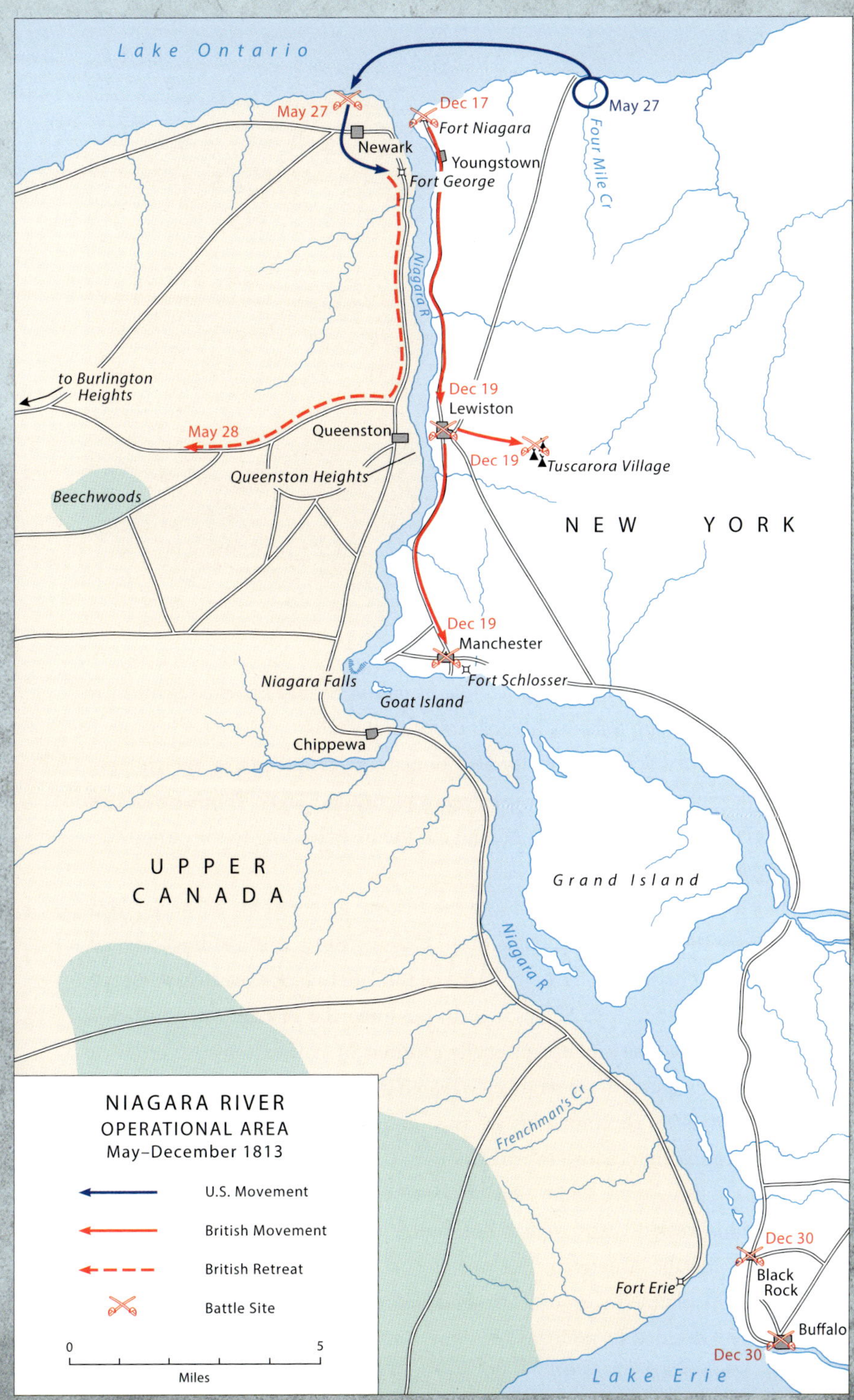

Lake Ontario
May 27
Dec 17
Fort Niagara
Newark
Youngstown
Fort George
Four Mile Cr
May 27
Niagara R
to Burlington Heights
Dec 19
Lewiston
May 28
Queenston
Dec 19
Tuscarora Village
Queenston Heights
Beechwoods
NEW YORK
Dec 19
Manchester
Niagara Falls
Fort Schlosser
Goat Island
Chippewa
UPPER CANADA
Grand Island
Niagara R
Frenchman's Cr
NIAGARA RIVER
OPERATIONAL AREA
May–December 1813
U.S. Movement
British Movement
British Retreat
Battle Site
0
5
Miles
Dec 30
Black Rock
Fort Erie
Buffalo
Dec 30
Lake Erie
Map 2

◄ *Capture of Fort George,* engraving by Alonzo Chappel. (Library of Congress)

main gate, the magazine exploded. A piece of falling timber knocked Scott from his mount, causing him to break his collarbone in the fall.

Despite his injury, Scott entered the abandoned fort, found an axe, and chopped down the flagpole to claim the British flag. Meanwhile, Capts. Thomas Stockton and Jacob Hindman rushed past Scott and cut the fuses leading to the gunpowder stored in each bastion. (See Map 2.)

Scott turned his attention to pursuing the British, gathered his advance guard, and set off on the road toward Queenston. Colonel Burn and his dragoons had been delayed in crossing the river and arrived too late to block the British escape. Burn eventually joined with Scott's men in pursuing the British. Morgan Lewis, unaware of the situation and exceptionally cautious by nature, sent two orders to Scott to call off the pursuit. General Lewis feared that Scott risked defeat if Vincent turned to fight. Scott continued his advance until General Boyd caught up with him and ordered him to return to Fort George.

There was nothing more to do; General Vincent managed to escape, and within days he and his weak division were at Burlington Heights.

Upon learning the American fleet was at Fort George, Governor General Sir George Prevost planned a riposte. He and his naval commander, Commodore Sir James Yeo, decided to raid the key American naval base at Sackett's Harbor to capture what naval stores they could and to destroy the shipbuilding facilities and any vessels under construction. They understood that the defense of Upper Canada was impossible if the Americans gained naval superiority on Lake Ontario.

On the evening of May 27, Yeo's squadron towed nine hundred soldiers in thirty-three bateaux and other small craft onto the lake and headed for the American base. The wind was weak, and on the following day, the British squadron was still approaching Sackett's Harbor. American picket ships spotted the British and sailed back to sound the alarm. The senior American officer at Sackett's Harbor, Col. Electus Backus of the 1st Regiment of Light Dragoons, had only 313 dragoons, 142 artillerymen, and 167 men of the Albany Volunteers to defend the base. He therefore sent word to the local militia commander, Brig. Gen. Jacob J. Brown, who ordered out the county militia before riding to Sackett's Harbor from his home eight miles away. Additionally, there were over three hundred wounded and sick in the hospital in Fort Volunteer.

Prevost knew that he had lost the element of surprise and contemplated aborting the mission. However, the British saw a number of bateaux carrying soldiers along the shore toward Sackett's Harbor. These were about two hundred fifty American recruits. The wind shifted direction sufficiently for Prevost to send a gunboat and about forty Indians in canoes to intercept the American bateaux. The Americans, hearing the yells and seeing the Indians in their war paint, pulled for shore and fled into the forest. The natives followed, and in an uneven battle, killed over twenty Americans at the cost of just a single warrior. Over one hundred fifteen Americans then reboarded their boats and paddled out to the British fleet to offer their

▼ These re-enactors give an impression of camp life on campaign during the War of 1812. While a summer camp could be relatively pleasant and airy, winter camps could be miserable and disease-ridden affairs. (Corvair Owner/CC BY-SA 2.0)

surrender rather than to fall into the hands of the Indians. For the Americans, the battle for Sackett's Harbor was off to a shaky start. Encouraged by his easy victory over the recruits, Prevost decided to go ahead with the attack. The next morning, at dawn on May 29, the British came ashore on Horse Island, continuously under fire from the Albany Volunteers. As more British infantry landed, the Albany Volunteers broke contact and withdrew across the causeway that linked the island to the mainland. They took up a position to the right of General Brown and several hundred militiamen. Brown had placed his citizen-soldiers behind a natural breastwork to give them cover and confidence. The militia and volunteers opened fire as the British rushed across the narrow path between the island and the mainland. The militia fired a ragged volley and then quickly withdrew without orders. Brown was furious. He desperately tried to rally his scattering command, taking him temporarily out of the battle. Fortunately for the Americans, the wind was so weak that only three British vessels could work their way close enough to

▼ *South-east view of Sackett's harbour*, by T. Birch. At its peak of shipbuilding productivity during the War of 1812, the shipyard employed some 3,000 workers. (Library of Congress)

shore to add their firepower to the battle. Meanwhile, the Albany Volunteers linked up with the regulars under Colonel Backus. Both groups slowly withdrew toward the barracks at Basswood Cantonment, where they stood and fought it out.

British and American regulars exchanged a heavy fire in which Colonel Backus fell mortally wounded. Command of the regulars and volunteers devolved upon Maj. Jacint Laval of the light dragoons. The British made several assaults on the barracks and nearby Fort Tompkins but were thrown back each time. To their great credit, a body of militia under the leadership of Capt. Samuel McNitt rallied and rejoined the fight. In the confusion, an American naval officer ordered the burning of the shipyard and the nearly completed ship, *General Pike*. Brown confronted another body of wavering militiamen and successfully directed them back into battle. Prevost saw the shipyard on fire, and sensing the futility of continuing the attack against stiff American resistance, ordered his forces to return to their boats. As the British withdrew, the Americans turned their attention to putting out the

fires. The British had suffered more than 250 casualties, while the Americans recorded 156 casualties on the twenty-ninth and nearly 140 more on the day before. Colonel Backus died eight days after the battle. Brown had missed much of the desperate fighting while rallying straggling militiamen. Nonetheless, the duty of writing the battle report fell to him as did the glory of the victory. Seven weeks later, the President named Brown a brigadier general in the Regular Army. Chauncey and his squadron returned to Sackett's Harbor a few days after the battle and contemplated just how close the British had come to destroying the shipyard and its hoard of naval stores. Never again would Chauncey leave his base at risk.

Shorn of naval support after Chauncey's withdrawal, Dearborn's army suffered two major setbacks that effectively doomed the 1813

campaign to clear the British from the Niagara region. The first setback, the nighttime battle of Stoney Creek, evolved from Dearborn's belated attempt to pursue the British force that had escaped after the fight for Fort George. Dearborn was very ill and his handling of the campaign reflected muddled thinking. General Winder, the Baltimore lawyer, lobbied hard to get command of the pursuing force. The cautious Dearborn eventually gave Winder what he wanted.

Winder started out on June 1, marching his seventeen hundred men along the narrow plain between the escarpment and Lake Ontario. Several creeks and ravines cut his line of march, while a handful of Indians and Canadian militiamen shadowed the column. By the next day, Winder's advance guard reached Forty Mile Creek, so named because it was that distance from the mouth of the Niagara River to the east. Dearborn, unsure of British strength, ordered former blacksmith John Chandler to take his brigade and join Winder. Chandler outranked Winder and would take command. On June 5, Chandler's brigade caught up to Winder's just west of Stoney Creek, a minor stream emptying into Lake Ontario. The American advance guard under Capt. Jacob Hindman had aggressively pushed back a British picket. This small engagement gave the Americans confidence but caused dismay in the British camp.

Chandler chose a good location for the two brigades. The left flank was anchored by the escarpment and the right flank by a swamp. However, he allowed his

▲ A marksman re-enactor fires his flintlock rifle. Note the two emissions of smoke: one from the muzzle and one from the pan, plus the debris produced by the disintegrating paper cartridge wad. (Maksim Sokolov [maxergon.com]/ CC BY-SA 4.0)

subordinate commanders to choose the positions of their bivouacs, resulting in a patchwork of unit campsites. A battery of guns covered the main road, but with no infantry within supporting distance. The 25th U.S. Infantry encamped about two hundred yards forward of the rest of the army. These soldiers started a number of campfires and began cooking supper when their regimental commander, Lt. Col. Joseph Lee Smith, ordered the men to pull back closer to their comrades. The men obeyed, leaving their fires burning. Smith's decision probably saved his men from being overrun in the ensuing battle. Unfortunately, he moved without informing Captain Hindman, whose advance guard battalion was posted on Smith's right flank. For other security, Chandler had deployed a rifle company as a picket west

▶ John Norton was the product of a Scottish mother and a Cherokee father. In his extraordinary life, he became the Mohawk chief Teyoninhokarawen and led major Native American forces against the Americans in the War of 1812, including at the battle of Stoney Creek. (Yale Center for British Art)

of the camp. The riflemen posted a few sentries, with the rest asleep in a church building. Chandler had also dispatched eight hundred soldiers of the 13th and 14th U.S. Infantry to guard the supply boats on the lake shore. This left him with about two thousand men at the main encampment.

Numerous members of the command later commented on the faulty arrangement of their camp. Lt. Ephraim Shaler, in his memoir, critiqued Chandler's decision to allow each unit to choose its own position.

> This was a great military blunder and the first I had discovered since we left Fort George. Being in an enemy's country and within a few miles of a large body of well disciplined troops (besides militia and Indians, who had been hanging about U.S. all day, though generally at a respectful distance) the whole brigade should have been encamped in regular military order, having a rallying point designated by the commanding General, to be understood by every commandant of a regiment; but unhappily for us, no such point was designated.

Despite their commander's error, many of the regimental officers fully expected to be attacked in the darkness, and they directed their soldiers to sleep with their weapons loaded.

British General John Vincent and his small division were only twelve miles away, perched on Burlington Heights. Vincent was in a difficult spot. Food and ammunition were both in short supply, and the Americans heavily outnumbered

▲ This cannon from Fort St. John, Canada, is mounted on a "Depression Carriage," a type of Garrison Carriage that enabled the gun to be fired, run out, and reloaded with the muzzle in a downward trajectory. (Tuchodi/CC BY-SA 2.0)

his force. However, he had to hold his position for as long as possible because it guarded the supply line to Maj. Gen. Henry Procter's division around Detroit. Loss of Burlington Heights would lead to the loss of all British holdings west of Lake Ontario. Vincent's second in command, the very able Lt. Col. John Harvey, scouted the American camp. He discovered the haphazard layout and reported this to Vincent. Until this time, Vincent believed that he had only two options, either to defend Burlington Heights in an unequal battle the following day or to withdraw back to York. Harvey, and others, suggested a third option, a night attack on the American camp. Vincent reluctantly agreed. Night attacks were notoriously risky, but all of his options were uncertain.

▶ *Color Bearer of the 25th U.S. Infantry, by Don Troiani. (Don Troiani Image Bank)*

Colonel Harvey took eight hundred infantrymen and a handful of Indian warriors and stealthily approached the American camp. He cautioned his soldiers not to make any sounds that might alert the Americans. The British had even removed the flints from their muskets so that no weapon could accidentally discharge. Along the way, the British captured or bayoneted at least three sentinels. They surrounded the church containing the sleeping picket guard and quietly captured Lt. Henry Van

Swearingen and twenty-five of his riflemen. At 0220 on June 6, the British assault columns came close enough to the American camp to see the campfires left burning by the 25th U.S. Infantry. Believing that they had caught the Americans by surprise, several of the attackers cheered as they moved forward. An American sentinel fired his musket and withdrew to the nearest American unit. The Americans quickly formed their lines as the British moved through the abandoned camp and realized their error.

Now the British were at the disadvantage. Backlit by the campfires, the British were easily seen by the Americans, who were themselves still in darkness. As the first American volleys tore into their ranks, the British were frantically returning the flints to their firelocks. The billowing smoke from the American muskets and cannon soon provided concealment for both sides. The natives allied to the British, as well as many British soldiers, let loose frightening yells. This terrorized many of the Americans; the memory of the Raisin River Massacre was still fresh on their minds. Eight-year-old Elizabeth Gage, in whose house several officers had taken up quarters, recalled many years later, "The officers rushed out of the house when the noise commenced and soon some of the soldiers came running in. I well remember how scared they were. They thought it was the Indians, from the yelling, and were afraid of being tomahawked." Captain Hindman's

◄ War of 1812 re-enactors depicting U.S infantry (and British battlefield dead) release a volley of shots. Battlefields of this age were intensely smoky affairs, with vision seriously reduced by smoke obscuration, particularly when artillery was used. (Skeezix1000/CC BY-SA 2.0)

advance guard of about three hundred men was caught forward of the main body of Americans. Unaware that Colonel Smith had pulled back a few hours earlier, Hindman held his ground. General Winder, not knowing that there were still Americans forward of the artillery, saw the activity and decided that this was a body of British. He ordered the artillery to fire into Hindman's men with canister. Charged in the front by a line of British bayonets and receiving deadly fire from their own artillery in the rear, Hindman's soldiers withdrew as best they could.

Meanwhile, the outnumbered British could not make an impression on the main American line. They charged the 25th U.S. Infantry at least three times and were thrown back by volleys of musketry. Many of the British soldiers began slipping quietly in the dark toward the rear and relative safety. Then, a chain of events occurred that tipped the scales in favor of the King's men. Chandler, riding frantically from unit to unit, was thrown from his horse and knocked unconscious. Coming to but shaken, he limped toward his artillery unit to direct its fire. The artillery was in the center of the American line but was still unsupported by infantry. For some unknown reason, the artillerymen had no muskets with them. Maj. Charles Plenderleath, commander of the British 49th Regiment of Foot, found himself a short distance from the American guns as they discharged. Plenderleath, on horse, ordered a bayonet assault and led fewer than thirty infantrymen at a dead run directly toward the American cannon, hoping to reach them before they fired again.

▼ A fine example of a blockhouse built in Canada during the War of 1812. This particular building stands on the waterfront at St. Andrews, New Brunswick, and was one of three built by locals as a defense against American raids. (Judith Bourque/CC BY-SA 2.0)

The impact was horrific. Unable to defend themselves from British steel, the unarmed American gunners fled, died, or surrendered. General Chandler, not realizing that the guns were now in enemy hands, staggered into the swarm with sword in hand and was quickly captured. Within minutes, General Winder and his staff rode up to the guns in the darkness. Winder was about to direct the fire of the artillery when British soldiers surrounded and captured him.

In the few remaining hours of darkness, firing slackened and eventually ceased. The British gathered their wounded and prisoners and trudged back to Burlington Heights. American regimental commanders, eager to receive orders from their brigade commanders, heard nothing and therefore did nothing. They did not learn that their generals were missing until the next morning. Command devolved upon Colonel Burn of the light dragoons. While personally brave, Burn was entirely unsuited for the task at hand. The American brigades were still more or less intact and in possession of the battlefield, yet he ordered a withdrawal to Forty Mile Creek.

At this point, Commodore Chauncey's decision to remain at Sackett's Harbor came into play. Royal Navy Commodore Yeo brought a small squadron from Kingston to see the situation at Fort George for himself. The feverish Dearborn was alarmed to learn that British vessels were sailing near the mouth of the Niagara.

With most of his army forty miles away, he feared that Yeo was about to land a force to retake Fort George. He ordered the army to return to Fort George. Yeo's ships harried the American withdrawal by attacking the column's supply boats until the force finally reached Fort George on June 9.

After the battle of Stoney Creek, Lt. Joseph Hawley Dwight recorded in his journal his frustration at the incompetence of his superior officers. "Here we saw the blessed effects of having plough joggers for generals whose greatest merits consist of being warm partisans and supporting administration right or wrong." Dwight was not the only disgruntled soldier. Many believed that their commanders had demonstrated shortcomings and a fatal lack of resolve.

Within weeks, a second disaster shocked the Americans and threw them back onto the defensive for the remainder of the year. Dearborn, still too ill to lead effectively, appointed General Boyd as his second in command. The British, augmented with several hundred Indian warriors, successfully bottled up the Americans in Fort George. Desirous to seize the initiative once again, Dearborn directed Boyd to seize a British outpost, the DeCew House. Lt. James FitzGibbon, leader of a highly effective British guerrilla band, made his headquarters at this location, roughly ten miles southwest of Queenston. Boyd gave the mission to conduct the raid to Lt. Col. Charles G. Boerstler, commander of the 14th U.S. Infantry. Lt. Col. Cyrenius Chapin and his guerrilla band of American mounted volunteers guided Boerstler's battalion. Boerstler and Chapin could hardly tolerate one another. Nonetheless, the American force started out on June 23 and reached Queenston after dark.

Early the next morning, Boerstler's command of about five hundred regulars of the 14th U.S. Infantry and two dozen of Chapin's volunteers climbed the escarpment and picked up a trail heading toward the DeCew House near the village of Beaver Dams. A small force of Indians under the command of Dominique Ducharme ambushed the Americans as they passed through a forest known locally

▲ This simple and solemn memorial to the battle of Beaver Dams was erected in 1874 (the photograph is from 1905) and marked the site where the bodies of 16 American soldiers were discovered. The stone was moved to the Battle of Beaverdams Park in 1976. (Archives of Ontario)

as the Beechwood. The confused fighting lasted for three hours as the warriors surrounded the Americans. Boerstler's men were running out of ammunition and Boerstler himself was wounded in the thigh. British Lieutenant FitzGibbon eventually arrived at the battle and approached the Americans under a flag of truce. He told Boerstler that he would be unable to prevent a massacre unless Boerstler surrendered immediately. The bluff worked. The Americans had suffered about thirty killed and another fifty wounded. Unable to break free of the ambush and fearing a slaughter, Boerstler agreed to surrender his command. The battle of Beaver Dams ended as the 14th U.S. Infantry trudged off to captivity.

Fed up with Dearborn's lack of success, Secretary Armstrong moved him to a quiet command in New York City and appointed General Wilkinson to replace him. The American army on the Niagara Peninsula, demoralized by defeat and now riddled with disease, barely managed to hold on to Fort George while it awaited its new commander.

Defending the Northwest

January–August 1813

The loss of Brig. Gen. James Winchester's brigade on the River Raisin in January 1813 shattered William Henry Harrison's plans to recapture Detroit. The short battle had cost the Americans nearly nine hundred men killed or captured. Fewer than one hundred had evaded capture to return to American lines. Encouraged by the series of British victories in late 1812 and early 1813, the Indians of the Northwest Territory drove American settlers eastward. The Shawnee chief, Tecumseh, provided vision and charismatic leadership to this revived native movement.

Other factors forced General Harrison to adopt a defensive posture, at least temporarily. His militia forces would reach the end of their short term of service in February and March, leaving him with only some regulars and twelve-month volunteers. British naval forces controlled Lake Erie, at least until summer when Perry's fleet being built at Erie might be ready to challenge them. Therefore, supplies for Harrison's army had to be moved by land and river, always a challenge on the frontier. The thawing roads were impassible for wagons and artillery, and supply columns were always under the threat of ambush. Harrison

▼ This portrait of Maj. Gen. William H. Harrison appeared in an 1824 book that declared itself a "vindication of his character and conduct as a statesman, a citizen, and a soldier." At this stage of his life, Harrison was actually suffering from severe financial hardship. (University of Pittsburgh Library)

decided to plan the 1813 campaign with deliberation and solid preparation. To that end, he determined to construct a large base of operations on the south bank of the Maumee River, not far from where that river entered Lake Erie. Harrison was well served in this endeavor by Capt. Eleazar Wood, a particularly energetic and skilled engineer and a graduate of the United States Military Academy.

Wood laid out a fortification on high ground about three hundred yards from the river. The fort enclosed eight acres and consisted of seven blockhouses and five batteries connected by a high timber palisade. Captain Wood directed workers to build two traverses inside the fortification. Each traverse was a continuous earthen wall, ten feet in height, which would limit the damage of artillery rounds landing inside the fort. Wood wrapped the two ammunition magazines in earthen walls for added protection. The Americans mounted twenty artillery pieces in the batteries, including four 18-pounder cannon, heavy pieces for frontier work. Harrison named the complex Fort Meigs, in honor of the governor of Ohio, whose citizens were protected by the new fort.

On April 25, British General Procter departed Fort Amherstburg on the Detroit River with nearly one thousand regulars and militia. On April 27, he united with Tecumseh, who had brought nearly fourteen hundred Indian warriors to the Maumee River. The two leaders decided on a formal siege of Fort Meigs. The following day, in a rainfall, the British prepared four battery positions on the left bank of the river opposite the American fort. Tecumseh positioned his forces south of the river to encircle the American position. The British brought eight artillery pieces with them, including two 24-pounder guns. Over the next few days, they threw nearly one thousand rounds into the fort. This heavy fire killed seven

▶ Artillery defends the perimeter at the modern Fort Meigs historic site, demonstrating the ingenuity of military carpenters in creating defensible positions. (Triple Tri/CC BY 2.0)

▼ A vintage (1901) map of Lake Erie, prepared by the War Department, Corps of Engineers. Although the smallest (by water volume) of the Great Lakes, Erie is still a sizeable body of water, measuring 241 miles long and 57 miles wide at its maximum width. (Toledo-Lucas County Public Library)

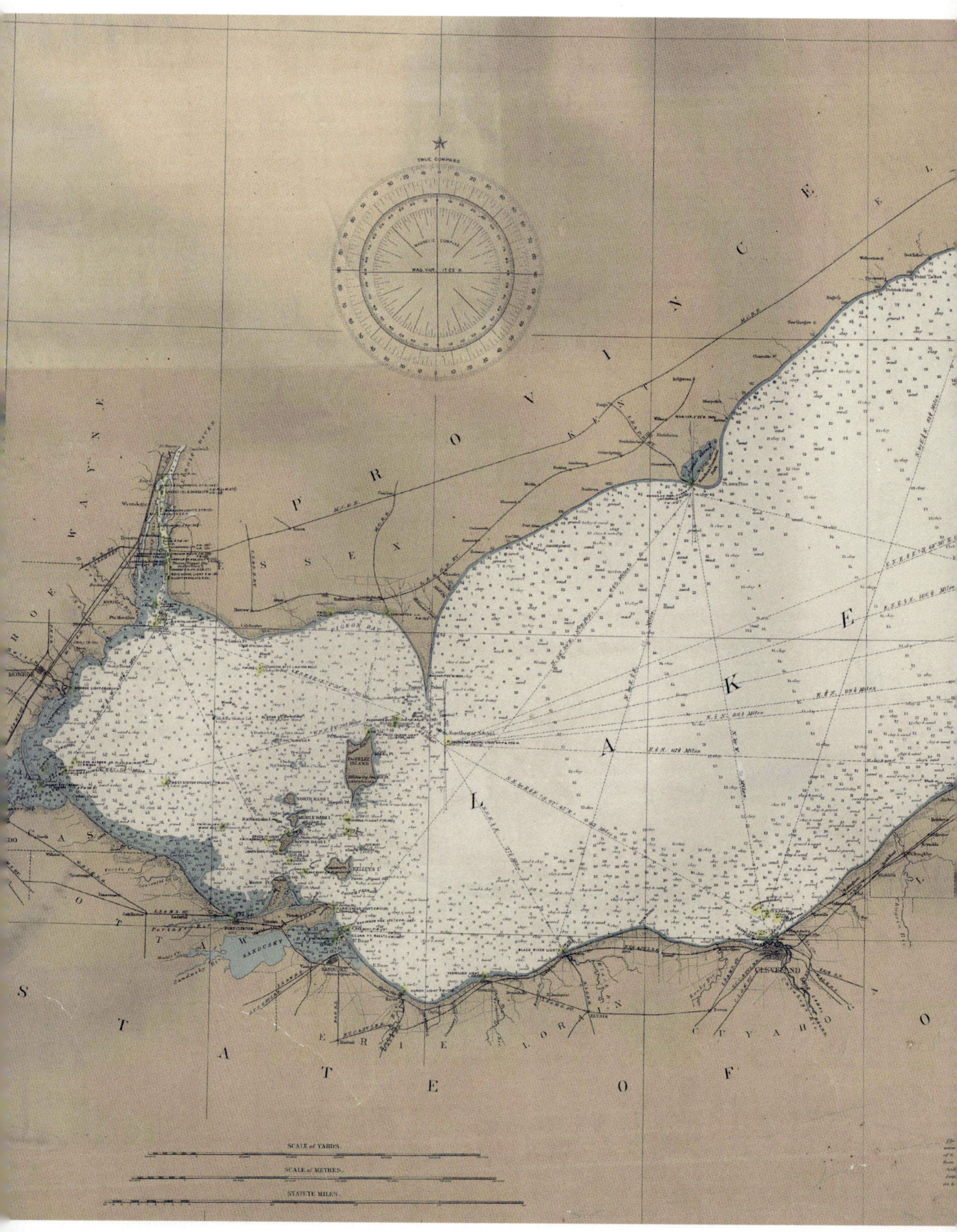

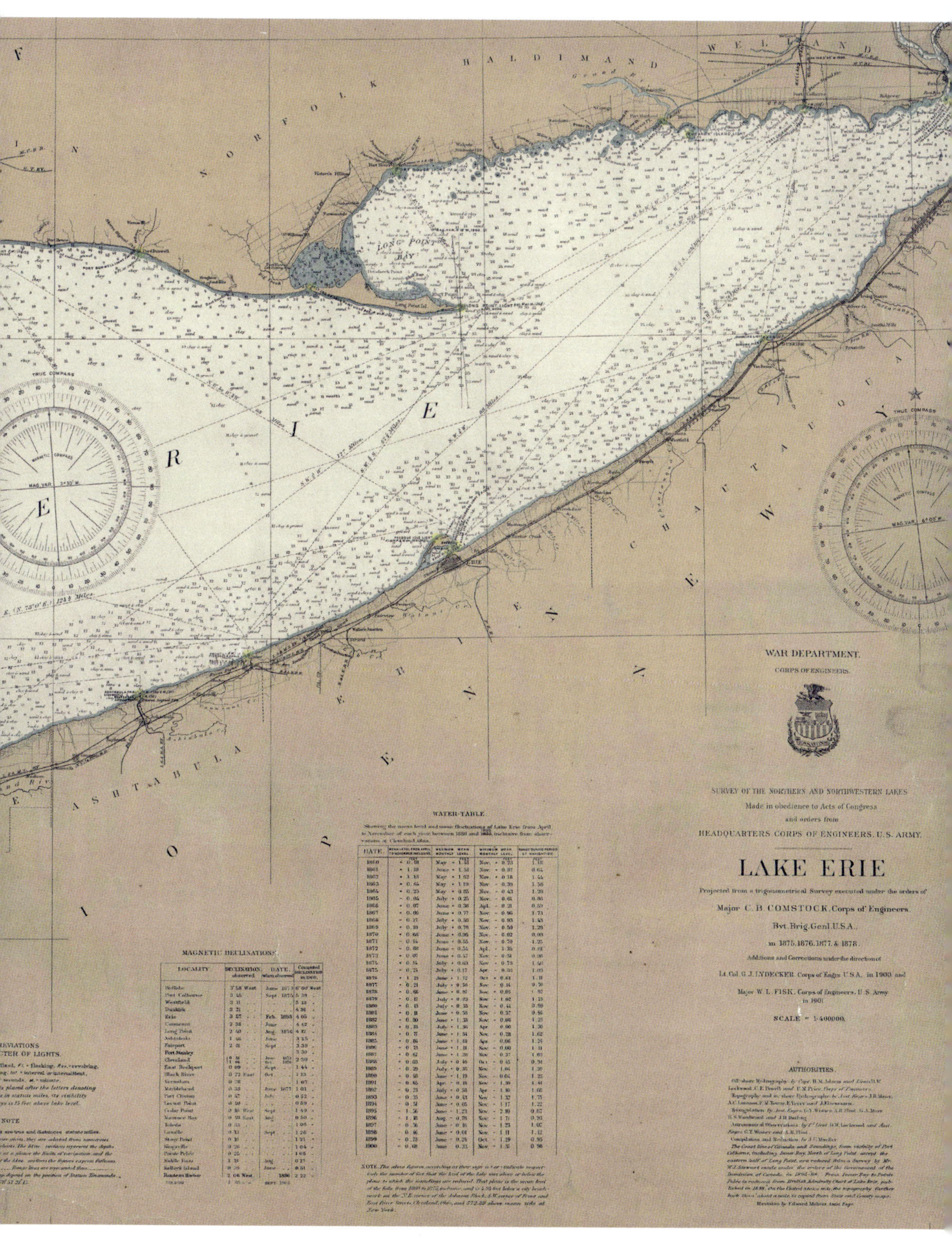
WAR DEPARTMENT.
CORPS OF ENGINEERS.
SURVEY OF THE NORTHERN AND NORTHWESTERN LAKES
Made in obedience to Acts of Congress
and orders from
HEADQUARTERS CORPS OF ENGINEERS, U.S. ARMY.
LAKE ERIE
Projected from a trigonometrical Survey executed under the orders of
Major C. B. COMSTOCK, Corps of Engineers,
Bvt. Brig. Genl. U.S.A.
in 1875, 1876, 1877, & 1878.
Additions and Corrections under the direction of
Lt. Col. G. J. LYDECKER, Corps of Engrs. U.S.A., in 1900 and
Major W. L. FISK, Corps of Engineers, U.S. Army
in 1901
SCALE = 1:400000.
WATER-TABLE
MAGNETIC DECLINATIONS.
AUTHORITIES.
LAKE ERIE
HALDIMAND
WELLAND
NORFOLK
LONG POINT BAY
CHAUTAUQUA
ASHTABULA
TRUE COMPASS
MAGNETIC COMPASS

Americans and wounded seventeen others, light casualties for the intensity of the cannonade. The Americans, who were short on artillery ammunition, set about recovering some of the shot that had landed in the fort. The armorers issued a measure of whiskey for each recovered cannon ball, a powerful incentive for the men under siege.

On May 3, the Americans discovered that the British had established a battery of guns on the southern side of the river only four hundred yards from the fort. Now the fort was in a cross fire. The men reacted quickly, throwing up shorter traverses at right angles to the new line of enemy fire. The following day, Procter demanded that Harrison surrender. With morale high and casualties low among the garrison, and with the knowledge that Kentucky militia under the command of Brig. Gen. Green Clay was coming down the river from Fort Defiance by flatboat, Harrison shrugged off the demand. When General Clay managed to get a message through that his Kentuckians were only a few hours away, Harrison devised a plan to break the siege. He sent Capt. John Hamilton through Indian lines to link up and deliver the plan to Clay.

General Harrison directed that two-thirds of the Kentucky militia, about eight hundred men, land on the north bank of the river and stealthily move toward the British batteries to spike the guns and destroy the gun carriages. Hamilton provided Clay with the necessary spikes. As soon as the Kentuckians silenced the

▼ Cannon from the War of 1812 seen at Amherstburg, Ontario, one freezing January. Winter presented multiple challenges for gun crews, the problems ranging from damp powder and slippery ground (the latter problematic for recoil management) through to frozen tools and dangerously brittle barrels. (Andrea_44/CC BY 2.0)

four British batteries, they were to regain their boats and cross back to the south bank before the British in their nearby camp could react. The remainder of the Kentuckians, about four hundred, would land on the south side of the river and cut their way through the Indian warriors and reach the safety of the fort. Meanwhile, Harrison would assault and destroy the lone British battery on his side of the Maumee. The plan was solid, but the execution was not.

Early on May 5, Clay directed Lt. Col. William Dudley to lead his regiment in an assault of the British batteries, while Clay moved with Lt. Col. William Boswell's smaller regiment directly to Fort Meigs. Clay and Boswell's men fought their way through the native warriors and reached the fort, bringing their wounded with them. Dudley's regiment, however, headed for disaster. Dudley divided his men into three columns. The left column would quietly move around the batteries, interposing itself between the guns and the British camp beyond. The center column would form a reserve. Dudley would lead the right column directly to the guns. However, Dudley had not briefed his men thoroughly, particularly of the importance of moving to Fort Meigs as soon as the batteries were dealt with. Dudley's column assaulted the guns successfully without losing a man. The spikes were inexplicably missing, and Dudley's men vainly attempted to drive musket ramrods into the touchholes of the cannon. While Dudley's men fumbled in trying to destroy guns, the left column ran into enemy warriors and pursued them into the forest and out of range of the covering fire from the American guns in Fort Meigs. Rather than obey orders to return to Fort Meigs immediately after spiking the guns, Dudley instead followed his left column into the forest. Procter, learning that his batteries had been taken, immediately counterattacked (Map 3).

The American units entering the forest lost their cohesion as Indian warriors drew them deeper into a trap. The Indians killed Dudley and dozens of his men. Hundreds of Americans surrendered to the British in the hope of escaping the scalping knife. As the new prisoners were marched off toward the British camp, the Indians escaped control and began shooting and tomahawking the Kentuckians. The British guard proved insufficient to stop the massacre. At least forty Kentuckians died after their surrender. Although one British soldier died trying, Procter failed to stop the killing. When Tecumseh arrived on the scene and brought his men under control, he accused Procter of moral cowardice. Relations between the two were shaky from that moment forward.

Meanwhile, Col. John Miller of the 19th U.S. Infantry led a sortie of about three hundred fifty regulars, volunteers, and militia that successfully captured the battery on the southern side of the river. Tecumseh's warriors counterattacked, but Miller's men repelled their repeated assaults and returned to the fort with forty-one British prisoners. Miller lost thirty killed and nearly ninety wounded in the sharp battle.

NORTHWEST OPERATIONS
April 27–October 5, 1813
British Movement
British Retreat
Battle Site
0
25
50
Miles
MICHIGAN TERRITORY
Lake Huron
Lake St. Clair
Thames R
Moraviantown
Oct 5
Detroit
Sandwich
UPPER CANADA
Detroit R
Brownstown
Fort Amherstburg
River Raisin
Frenchtown
Lake Erie
Fort Miami
Perry's Naval Engagement
Sep 10
INDIANA TERRITORY
Maumee R
Fort Meigs
Apr 28–May 9
Jul 21–28
Aug 1
Fort Stephenson
Aug 1–2
Fort Seneca
Sandusky R
Fort Defiance
OHIO

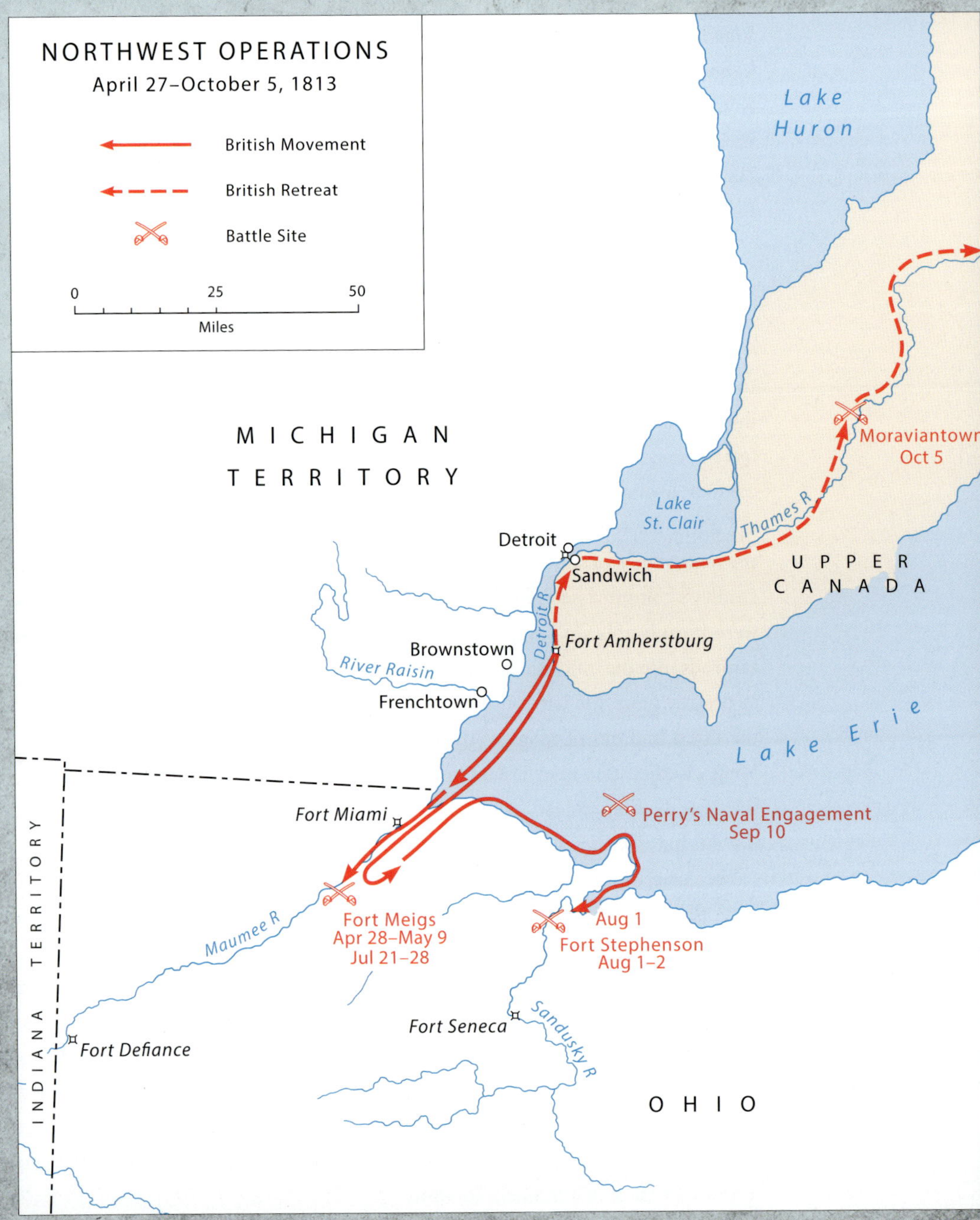

▲ Map 3

Despite destroying Dudley's regiment, Procter was unable to continue the siege. Tecumseh's Indians drifted away with the weapons and clothing looted from the Kentuckians. Canadian militiamen appealed to Procter to return home to plant corn. Dysentery and fever had thinned British ranks and supplies were running short. He therefore lifted the siege on May 9. Subsequent news of the American successes at York and Fort George further dampened Procter's likelihood of victory, while General Sheaffe refused to send reinforcements westward as he judged they were needed along Lake Ontario and the Niagara region.

Procter understood the overriding importance of control of Lake Erie in defending western Upper Canada. However, he was unwilling to gamble his slender force of regulars in an attack on the American squadron under construction at Erie. Instead, in July he gave in to Indian demands to renew the attack on Fort Meigs. This time, the American garrison was much stronger than in May. Having failed to lure the defenders out of the fort, Procter departed Fort Meigs and moved against Fort Stephenson, a small timber stockade fortification surrounded by a ditch, located on the Sandusky River. Maj. George Croghan of the 17th U.S. Infantry led about two hundred regulars in a determined defense. On August 1, Procter demanded the fort's surrender. Failure to capitulate, he warned, might result in a massacre by the Indians fighting alongside the British. Croghan refused. A British cannonade by three 6-pounder guns failed to

▼ This map depicts the layout of Fort Stephenson in 1813. At the time of the battle for the fort in August 1813, it was garrisoned by 160 U.S. troops led by Major George Croghan, who was the recipient of a Congressional Gold Medal. (Emilius Randall and Daniel J. Ryan)

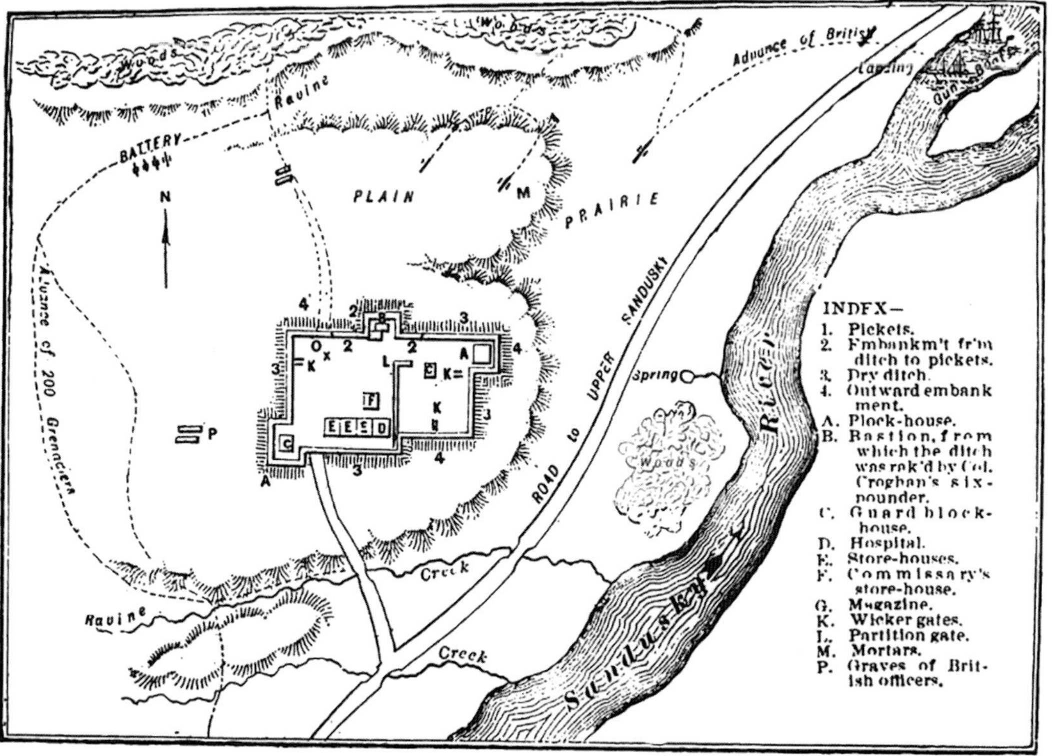

▲ Miller's Charge on May 5, 1813. (Anne S. K. Brown Military Collection)

breach the stockade. Nonetheless, the following day, Procter ordered an assault. The Indians who were supposed to join the attack failed to do so. American gunfire cut down British infantrymen in the ditch, and Procter called off the attack. The British suffered nearly one hundred casualties, including twenty-nine prisoners, while the defending Americans lost one soldier killed and seven wounded. Procter withdrew to lick his wounds. The British failure at Fort Stephenson marked the limit of their successes. The advantage was about to shift inexorably to Harrison, and the turning point proved the most decisive naval fight of the war.

The Offense, September–October 1813

In 1813, Master Commandant Perry directed a most improbable undertaking, the creation of a naval squadron from scratch on the shores of Lake Erie. Just as his superior Isaac Chauncey had engaged in a naval arms race with Sir James Yeo on Lake Ontario, Perry was in a desperate race to outbuild British Capt. Robert Heriot Barclay's squadron. Both Perry and Barclay were dependent on their leaders, Chauncey and Yeo, for every sailor, shipwright, cannon, sail, and cable. Barclay's vessels were stationed at the shipyard at Amherstburg on the Detroit River. After Fort George fell in May, American vessels at Black Rock on the Niagara River evaded the British and joined the rest of the Lake Erie squadron in Presque Isle Bay at Erie, Pennsylvania.

Although well protected from lake storms and British guns, Presque Isle Bay was nearly blocked at its mouth by an extensive sandbar. Allowing only six feet of draft, the sandbar prevented Perry's brigs from leaving the bay when loaded with cannon and stores. At the end of July, Perry was ready to move, and as luck would have it, just as Barclay's squadron, which had been blockading the harbor, moved off. The Americans sent their smaller craft into the lake to protect the effort of the larger ships to cross the sand obstacle as best they could. Perry's men off-loaded the guns and rigging from the brigs *Lawrence* and *Niagara* and attached water-filled containers called camels to the sides of the *Lawrence*. As water was pumped out of the camels, the *Lawrence* rose in the water. Crews dragged the *Lawrence* across the wide sandbar and into deep water. The Americans repeated the process with the *Niagara*.

The entire process took four days during which time the squadron was particularly vulnerable to attack. On August 4, with *Lawrence* still unarmed and *Niagara* only part way across the sandbar, Barclay returned to Presque Isle. Had he attacked, the ensuing fight would have been one-sided. However, Barclay did

Profile:
Sir James Lucas Yeo (1782–1818)

Although the life of Sir James Yeo was cut short prematurely at the age of 35, he packed his time with an extraordinary density of exploits and accolades. He was born in the maritime city of Southampton, England, on October 7, 1782, the son of a naval victualling agent, and joined the Royal Navy as a midshipman at age 10. By 1796, he was the acting lieutenant commanding the 16-gun sloop *Albacore*; he made full lieutenant the following year.

Between the 1790s and the outbreak of the War of 1812, Yeo found constant adventure, despite battling repeated bouts of ill health, especially the yellow fever he contracted in the tropics. He was brought to public attention in 1805, when he led a group of just 50 men in the capture of two Spanish shore batteries at El Muros, Spain, garrisoned by more than 200 troops. During the action, he took only six casualties and captured the ship *Confiance*, which was taken into service under Yeo's command. Further audacious actions against the French in French Guiana in 1808 led to his award of the Military Order of Aviz by Portuguese Prince Regent João and the grant of the Order of the Bath by Britain's King George III.

In 1813, Yeo was appointed to take command of the Royal Navy fleet operating on the Great Lakes. Yet the strength of his American enemy and his poor relations with British Army General George Prevost hampered his fortunes in the theater. Following the war, he was posted to the coast of West Africa, hunting down slave ships. There his yellow fever resurfaced and he died on August 21, 1818, while sailing back to England.

◄ The original caption of this 1813 artwork reads: "United States sloop of war *General Pike*, commodore *Chauncey*, and the British sloop of war *Wolf*, Sir James Yeo, Preparing for action, September 28, 1813."

not realize the vulnerable state of the American squadron. Without his flagship, the sloop-of-war *Detroit*, which was not yet ready at the Amherstburg shipyard, Barclay did not believe he could successfully challenge Perry. He therefore drew off to consolidate his fleet. Perry quickly rearmed his brigs and set sail westward, looking to bring Barclay to battle.

At dawn on September 10, the Americans spotted six of Barclay's vessels. Perry gave the order to close, but the wind was against him. The American squadron consisted of the brigs *Lawrence* and *Niagara* and seven smaller vessels. Few crewmen in either fleet were fully trained sailors. Many were soldiers and recently recruited landsmen. Kentucky riflemen sat high in the rigging of the American ships to pick off officers aboard British ships. Perry had the advantage in firepower. His vessels had a combined broadside weight of 912 pounds, nearly twice that for Barclay's ships. Despite this advantage, the battle could easily have gone to Barclay.

In midmorning, the wind shifted in favor of the Americans. While the British vessels formed in line to await the Americans, Perry's squadron was strung out in a column a mile long. Perry aboard his flagship, *Lawrence*, ran up his battle flag, a blue pennant emblazoned with the immortal words of naval hero James Lawrence, "Don't Give Up the Ship." Trailing astern came *Niagara* commanded by Master Commandant Jesse D. Elliott. Shortly after noon, *Lawrence* came into reach of the long-range guns of three of Barclay's vessels. For the next two hours, *Lawrence* fought for survival in an uneven contest. For some inexplicable reason, Elliott hung back out of the fight. Every officer aboard *Lawrence* except Perry was killed or wounded and few guns were still firing. Perry knew that the only way to win this battle was to bring *Niagara* into action. He climbed into a ship's boat and a crew rowed him through a hail of bullets and cannon shot over to *Niagara*. He took command of *Niagara* and quickly reengaged Barclay's larger vessels. The British squadron could not fend off *Niagara* with its fresh guns and crew. By 1500, the wounded Barclay surrendered his squadron. Perry returned to the stricken *Lawrence* and was greeted with three cheers from the survivors. He wrote a message to Harrison: "We have met the enemy and they are ours: Two Ships, two Brigs, one Schooner & one Sloop." Conditions were now ripe for Harrison's advance to retake Detroit.

Henry Procter well understood that the loss of the British squadron left his forces vulnerable if the Americans attacked. Barclay's boats had transported supplies across the length of Lake Erie. Now, supplies were reduced to a trickle. Procter declared a limited martial law in western Upper Canada in order to seize food and wagons and to deal with disaffected citizens. He consulted with his immediate superior, Maj. Gen. Francis de Rottenburg, who had replaced General Sheaffe following the loss of York. After a flurry of exchanged letters, Procter secured permission to retreat eastward. Tecumseh, eventually learning that the British would be abandoning his native warriors, was incensed. Nonetheless, he agreed to move eastward with Procter along the Thames River, with an understanding that the combined force would make a stand.

General Harrison also understood the implications of Perry's victory and prepared for an offensive to destroy Anglo-Indian power in the region. By

September, he had the services of two regular brigades under the command of Brig. Gens. Lewis Cass and Duncan McArthur. Revolutionary War veteran and Kentucky Governor Isaac Shelby was moving quickly to join Harrison with three brigades of Kentucky militia. Harrison also had the services of a uniquely American military formation. Congressman Richard M. Johnson was commissioned a colonel and commanded a strong regiment of mounted Kentucky volunteers. Clad in long black hunting shirts and armed with an assortment of rifles, tomahawks, and hunting knives, these experienced frontier fighters gave Harrison a mobile shock force. Perry's squadron controlled Lake Erie, easing Harrison's logistical efforts and giving the Americans greater operational reach.

On September 27, Perry landed Harrison's infantry at the mouth of the Detroit River on the Canadian side just south of Fort Amherstburg. That same day, the British, their Indian allies, and hundreds of civilians had begun a slow retreat up the Detroit River to Lake St. Clair heading toward the mouth of the Thames River. Harrison's men entered Detroit on the twenty-ninth. Capt. Stanton Sholes, who commanded a company of the 2d Artillery, recalled, "A part of our Army Crossed over to Detroit. At our landing we were met by the Citizens men women and Children, on the shore. They manifested great Joy, at our timely arrival."

On October 2, Harrison set out after Procter. The British had a head start of nearly a week, yet their column,

◀ Still proud and patriotic, Oliver Hazard Perry stands at the bows of a small boat after abandoning his flagship, the *Lawrence*, during the battle of Lake Erie. The craft is being steered toward the *Niagara*. (Library of Congress)

Profile:
Native Americans in military service

The military history of the Native Americans between the 16th and the 19th centuries reflects the divided loyalties of the North American continent. Although they are popularly famous for their resistance to the colonizers, Native American tribes frequently sided with one or other of the European powers or with the inchoate U.S. federal state, as well as forming tribal confederacies. Their choice of side might stem from weary resignation to political realities, or as a means to gain advantages in trade, territory, or liberty.

From the early days of European colonization, Indians were used as scouts to assist in tracking, reconnaissance, navigation, and raiding. But later the Native Americans contributed major forces in the strategic struggles for the continent. During the French and Indian War (1754–63), for example, the bulk of the Algonquin-speaking tribes committed themselves to the French against the British, although the British did attract some Indian allies, particularly those of the Iroquois Confederacy. During the later War of Independence (1775–83), Native Americans again fought on opposing sides, although the balance of their loyalty leaned towards the British, who they regarded as a bulwark against the expansionist Americans.

The War of 1812 saw about 1,000 Native Americans serving with federal forces, ultimately formed into the Corps of Cherokee Indians. But again, the indigenous peoples largely sided with Britain, who came to depend heavily on Indian allies. Sadly for the Native Americans, their contribution ultimately did nothing to guarantee their security in North America.

▲ This Indian scout re-enactor displays the light and practical dress of the Native American warrior, perfect for both enduring the elements and moving easily through the woodlands of the American Northeast. (Corvair Owner/CC BY-SA 2.0)

burdened by heavy baggage, traveled slowly. To quicken their pace, the British burned excess weapons, ammunition, and food as they moved eastward along the Thames River. Harrison's forward patrols captured ammunition bateaux that had fallen behind in the retreat.

Learning that Harrison was closing rapidly, Procter chose to make his stand just west of the settlement at Moravian town. He placed his regulars on the left, while Tecumseh's native warriors occupied the right. The regulars were anchored by the river on their left and an extensive swamp on their right. Not having enough men to cover his front in strength, Procter placed his regulars in open order through nearly two hundred yards of open woods. A narrow swamp in front of the regulars helped shield their position. Tecumseh's position to the north was more protected. The Indians occupied the edge of a broad, heavily wooded swamp that ran generally parallel to the river. Because they were forward of the regulars, Tecumseh's warriors flanked any attack moving along the road to Moravian town.

▲ *William Henry Harrison, by Rembrandt Peale. (National Portrait Gallery, Smithsonian)*

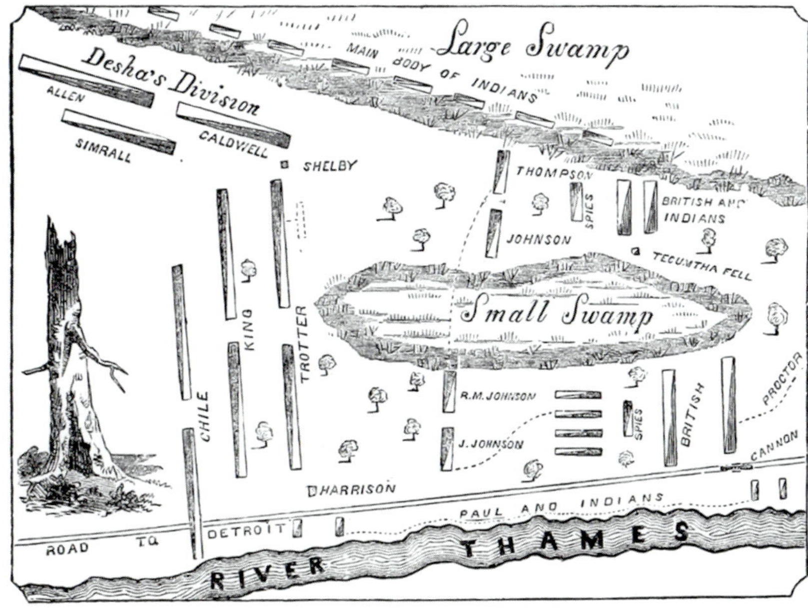

▶ A 19th-century map captures the forces and movements of the battle of the Thames. It clearly suggests how the location of swampland affected the opportunities for maneuver. (British Library)

After his engineer, Eleazar Wood, reconnoitered the enemy positions, Harrison decided to make his main attack against the British regulars, while a brigade of Kentucky militia faced Tecumseh's force in the great swamp. Harrison initially ordered Johnson and his mounted riflemen to move across the small swamp in front of the British regulars and to attack Tecumseh's left, where the

Col. Johnsons mounted men charging a party of British Artillerists and Indians, at when the whole of the British force commanded by Gen. Procter, surrendered to the Am

native warriors linked up with the right of the British line. Johnson offered a different course of action. He volunteered his regiment in an attack directly into the British regulars. Struck by this bold and unorthodox plan, Harrison agreed. Johnson ordered his brother and second in command, Lt. Col. James Johnson, to take half the regiment against the British line while he led the other half into Tecumseh's men.

Richard Johnson ordered the bugle to sound the advance. James Johnson's mounted riflemen moved through the woods quickly. The British infantry managed only a ragged volley before the mounted Kentuckians, yelling "Remember the Raisin," rode them down. This phase of the battle lasted less than ten minutes. Meanwhile, Colonel Johnson's men charged into Tecumseh's men in the swamp. Unable to navigate the wetlands on horse, Johnson's men dismounted. The Kentucky militia infantry joined the desperate fight. The battle in the wooded swamp lasted nearly an hour and was brutal in the extreme until Tecumseh was slain. Without their leader, the Indians faded into the forest.

No one can say for certain who killed Tecumseh. None of the Kentuckians had ever seen him in person. It is most likely that his followers took the body and buried it in the forest to keep it out of American hands. Johnson's men flayed the skin of a dead chieftain thought to be the great Shawnee leader and brought

◀ An 1813 engraving of the battle of Moravian Town shows U.S. cavalry under Colonel Johnson attacking British artillery positions and their Native American allies. Although formulaic to modern eyes, the artwork on closer inspection realistically suggests the brutality of close-quarters combat. (Dkutcher/CC BY-SA 4.0)

▼ *Remember the River Raisin!* by Ken Riley. (The National Guard series of the U.S. Army Center of Military History)

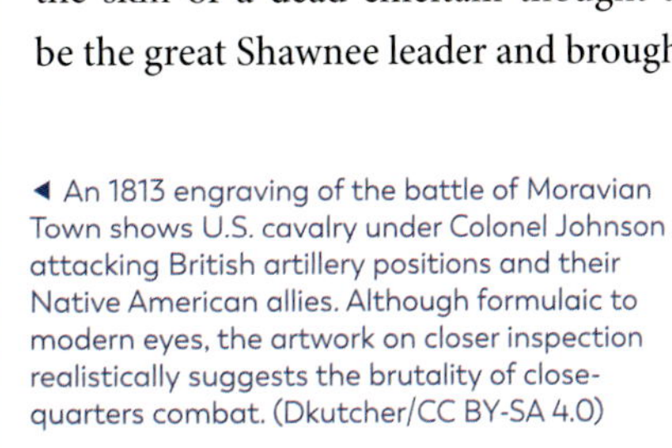

pieces of it back to Kentucky as souvenirs. Procter fled the battlefield after he saw his regulars break. About 250 British soldiers managed to withdraw back to Burlington Heights, but 634 were killed or captured.

Harrison's men found thirty-three Indian bodies and suspected that many more had been carried off. Only about four hundred natives withdrew with the British; the rest lost heart with the death of their leader and returned to their villages. Miraculously, Harrison lost only seven killed and twenty-two wounded. The

◄ *Battle of the Thames and the death of Tecumseh, by the Kentucky mounted volunteers led by Colonel Richard M. Johnson, 5th Oct. 1813,* by artist William Emmons. (Library of Congress)

Americans captured ten artillery pieces and recovered many of the battle flags lost at Detroit, River Raisin, and Fort Meigs.

Without sufficient provisions to pursue Procter's broken army, Harrison returned to Detroit. Within the next ten days, he dictated an armistice to the dispirited Indians. The Indians could return to their traditional lands but had to pledge peace, return all prisoners, and leave hostages as a guarantee of their future good behavior. The Americans provided food and other supplies to the natives. President Madison appointed Brig. Gen. Lewis Cass as governor of the Michigan Territory. Cass also governed that part of western Upper Canada that fell under American control. He allowed British officials willing to take an oath of fidelity to the United States during the occupation to continue in their civil offices. Harrison and Perry were celebrated throughout the United States for their decisive victories. As for Procter, Governor General Prevost ordered a court-martial for the losing commander. The court convicted Procter on several charges and suspended him from rank and pay for six months.

The Advance on Montreal, October–November 1813

American success in the West was not matched in the eastern theater. Indeed, the continued weaknesses in the U.S. Army in the second year of the war were nowhere so well illustrated than by the campaign to seize Montreal in the fall of 1813.

In March, Secretary Armstrong had ordered General Wilkinson, then at New Orleans, to report to General Dearborn. Wilkinson was a shady character. Although unproven at the time, he was suspected to be in the pay of Spanish authorities in Mexico to spy for them. He had also been deeply involved in Aaron Burr's prewar plot to build an empire from lands within the Louisiana Territory, but had managed to evade charges. Wilkinson's new command was the 9th Military District, comprising upstate New York, Vermont, and parts of Pennsylvania. His nemesis, Maj. Gen. Wade Hampton, was also assigned to the 9th Military District.

General Hampton, like Wilkinson a veteran of the Revolutionary War, was a successful politician and an enormously wealthy South Carolina planter. Hampton and Wilkinson had begun their feud before the war, and the small officer corps had been bitterly divided in its allegiance between them. Secretary Armstrong

promoted both men to major general on the same day, Wilkinson taking precedence. By summer, Hampton commanded the division of troops on Lake Champlain, while Wilkinson and Armstrong moved to Sackett's Harbor to devise a strategy. Hampton secured Armstrong's agreement that he would receive orders only from Armstrong, and not from Wilkinson. Hampton's men were largely new recruits. To his credit, he conducted a robust training regimen, although he was accused of condoning harsh discipline in order to gain results. Still, there were signs that all was not well in the training camps. Pvt. A. S. Cogswell of the 11th U.S. Infantry wrote in a letter to a friend:

> There is three of our officers appointed to inspect the flour, but they do not know good flour from Lime, therefore our Bread has been for some time (to speak politely about it) most damnable poor stuff, being made mostly of Rye flour, the other parts of our Rations are very good, except the whiskey.

Armstrong, Wilkinson, and Chauncey haggled over strategy. They considered three options. The first was to restart the floundering campaign on the Niagara Peninsula. The second was to capture Kingston, thus depriving the Royal Navy squadron of its essential base. The third choice was to seize Montreal, thus cutting off supplies and reinforcements to all British posts on the Great Lakes. Occupation of the Niagara Peninsula would not be decisive to the war effort. The choice boiled down to Kingston or Montreal. Chauncey preferred to take possession of Kingston, thus eliminating the British squadron. Armstrong and Wilkinson quibbled over the goal of the offensive, and in early October, Wilkinson seemed to consent to Kingston. Throughout the protracted process of deciding on a strategy, Wilkinson

▼ Logistics and movement in the Canadian wilderness required effort and ingenuity. Here an artillery battery use oxen to draw a field gun across a river. (British Library/PD)

was hampered by a debilitating illness. His physician treated him with laudanum, a mixture of opium and alcohol, which probably contributed to his cloudy judgment throughout the campaign. (See Map 4.)

Meanwhile, Hampton was not brought into the planning process. He was aware that his troops would contribute to the campaign, either by threatening Montreal while Wilkinson moved on Kingston or by joining Wilkinson somewhere on the St. Lawrence River for a combined thrust against Montreal. In September, Hampton marched his division of four thousand soldiers north across the border and rested at Odelltown. He apparently planned an advance on a route parallel to the Richelieu River, thus avoiding the major strongpoint at Isle aux Noix. However, he changed his mind because that line of advance would cross territory affected by drought and there would be insufficient water for men, horses, and cattle. Instead, he moved back south and then westward to Four Corners, New York (present-day Malone), on the Chateauguay River. The Chateauguay flowed northeast and entered the St. Lawrence opposite Montreal. Armstrong instructed Hampton to remain there to give Wilkinson more time to prepare for his end of the campaign.

Four weeks after he left Odelltown, Hampton received the order to proceed from Armstrong. Hampton's division advanced down the Chateauguay River on October 21, with Brig. Gen. George Izard as second in command. Nearly all of the fourteen hundred New York militiamen with him refused to cross the border. The remaining troops crossed into Canada, where they ran afoul of Lt. Col. Charles-Michel de Salaberry's French-speaking militia from Lower Canada.

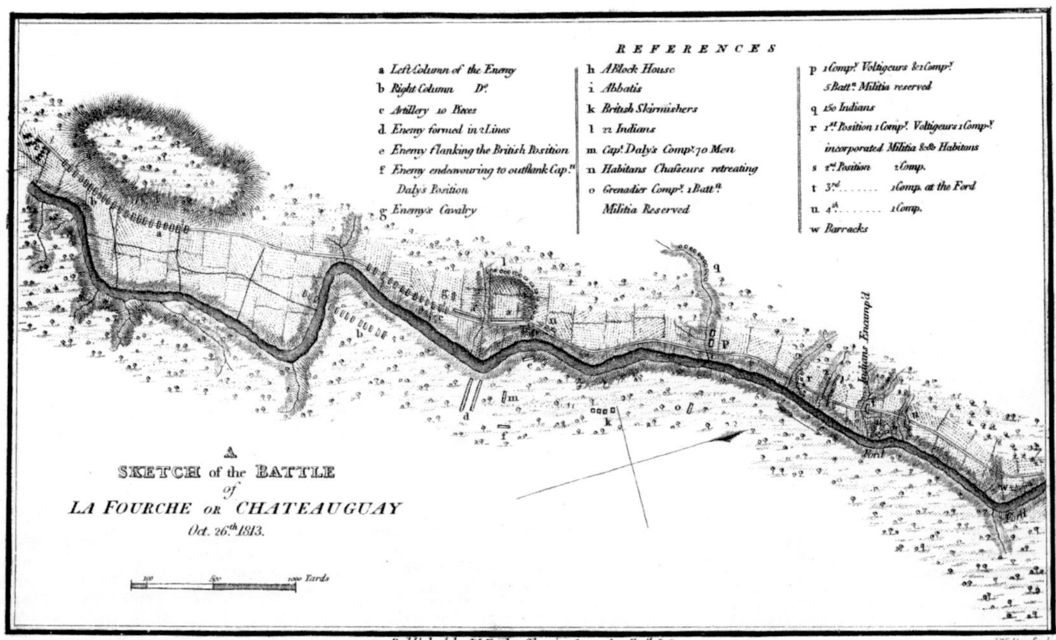

A detailed map created in 1815 shows the features and troop dispositions at the battle of Chateauguay, October 26, 1813. Fording points across the Chateauguay are marked on the far right. (Toronto Public Library)

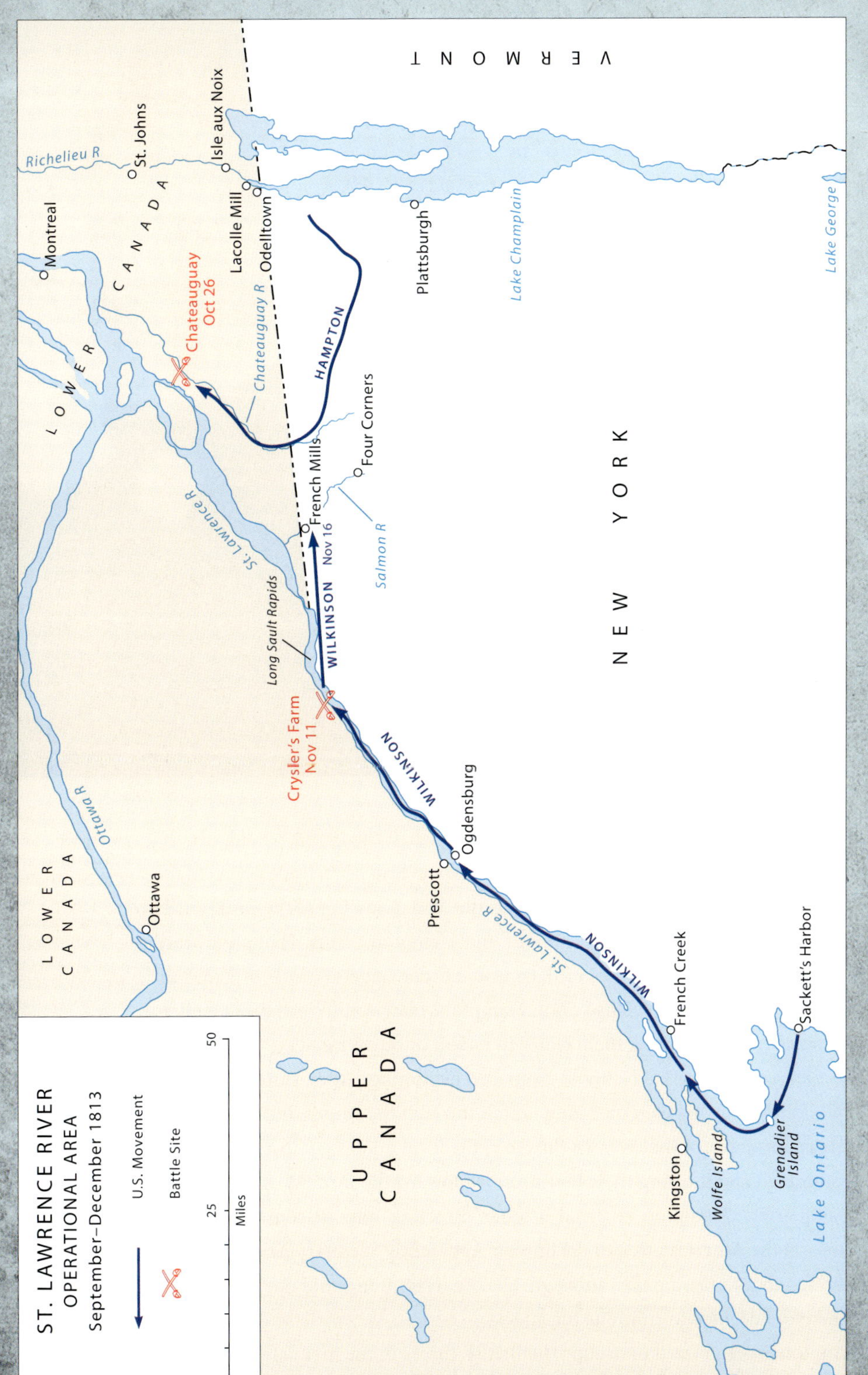
ST. LAWRENCE RIVER
OPERATIONAL AREA
September–December 1813

U.S. Movement
Battle Site

Miles
0   25   50

LOWER CANADA
UPPER CANADA
NEW YORK
VERMONT

Montreal
St. Johns
Isle aux Noix
Lacolle Mill
Odelltown
Richelieu R
Chateauguay R
Chateauguay
Oct 26
HAMPTON
Plattsburgh
Lake Champlain
Lake George
Four Corners
French Mills
Salmon R
Nov 16
WILKINSON
St. Lawrence R
Long Sault Rapids
Crysler's Farm
Nov 11
Ottawa R
Ottawa
Prescott
Ogdensburg
WILKINSON
St. Lawrence R
WILKINSON
French Creek
Kingston
Wolfe Island
Grenadier Island
Sackett's Harbor
Lake Ontario

▲ Map 4

On October 25, Hampton encountered a series of barricades and abatis that de Salaberry had erected to impede American progress. By interviewing the locals, he learned that there were essentially five defensive lines stretching nearly two miles along the river. The route through the British position was a road through a fairly dense forest.

Hampton needed the road to move his guns and supplies. Each defensive line consisted of a breastwork of dirt and timber built along a stream emptying into the river. The streambed served as a ditch, which strengthened the defensive value of the breastwork. The first defensive line was further strengthened by an abatis, which extended from the river's edge to a swamp several hundred yards into the forest.

Hampton understood that a direct assault through the strong British position would be costly. He learned that there was a ford across the Chateauguay located behind the last defensive line, and chose a risky strategy which, if successful, would turn the entire defensive line. He ordered Col. Robert Purdy to lead his brigade across to the right bank of the river and move directly to the ford. Crossing at the ford, Purdy would trap the defenders between himself and Hampton. When Hampton heard the firing coming from the distant ford, he would order General Izard's brigade into a frontal attack on the first defensive line. Hampton's plan would catch the defenders between two fires, prompting them either to retreat or be captured.

The plan came unraveled almost from the beginning. After sunset and in a rainfall, Purdy took his men on a long march through the woods and bogs on the right (eastern) bank of the river. In the dark, the local guides got lost and Purdy's men stumbled about trying their best to move toward the ford. Meanwhile, back at headquarters, Hampton received a letter directing him to construct winter quarters on the American side of the border. Apparently Secretary Armstrong was not serious about pressing the campaign. Shaken, Hampton could not recall Purdy and therefore decided to continue the attack.

Hampton ordered Izard to occupy the British forces in the first defensive line to draw their attention away from Purdy, who would supposedly arrive at the ford

▲ French Canadian officer Lieutenant Colonel Charles-Michel d'Irumberry de Salaberry joined the British Army when he was just 14. He built a solid reputation for fearless and intelligent leadership, most publicly confirmed in his victory at the battle of the Chateauguay in 1813. (Daderot/CC0 1.0)

soon. Izard ordered the 10th U.S. Infantry forward toward the abatis, and with some difficulty, deployed them on line. The regiment marched to the ravine and opened a brisk fire on de Salaberry's men positioned behind the abatis. The 10th maintained fire until it ran low on ammunition. On the opposite side of the river, Purdy heard the firing and oriented his men to move forward. He sent out an advance guard of two companies to feel their way through the thick woods, but they encountered some warriors and a company of militia. The two sides opened fire and sustained the firefight for perhaps fifteen minutes. With very poor visibility, both sides believed they were outnumbered and withdrew. The Canadian militia fell back upon another company of militia, and the combined forces cautiously moved forward to reestablish contact with the Americans. Purdy received exaggerated reports from his advance guard and an order from Hampton to break off the attack and return to the west side of the river. He rallied his men together as best he could in preparation for a withdrawal. Meanwhile, Izard brought up his entire brigade to support the 10th U.S. Infantry in front of de Salaberry's line.

Izard formed his three battalions into line and advanced on the British position. De Salaberry posted a skirmish line of three companies in front of the abatis. The Americans stood in ranks shoulder to shoulder and fired volleys at the Canadians who were hiding behind trees and rocks and firing independently. The Canadian fire proved quite accurate but could not prevail against the sheer volume of the American musketry. De Salaberry pulled his skirmishers back behind the abatis and Izard advanced. The intense firefight resumed. Soon the Canadians sent their

► This photograph of the battlefield at Chateauguay, taken in August 1926, gives a rather haunting impression of the terrain the two sides had to negotiate in battle in 1813. (Archives of Ontario)

Indian allies into the woods on the western side of the fight along with several buglers blowing a charge. To Izard, the signs were ominous; he believed the British were outflanking the American left.

Meanwhile, on the opposite side of the river, the two Canadian companies made contact with Purdy's much larger force in the woods and opened a brisk fire, which the Americans returned. Neither side knew the strength of the other. Eventually the Canadians withdrew out of range but re-formed and moved forward yet again. Outnumbered nearly twenty to one, the two Canadian militia companies charged the ragged line of Americans in the dense underbrush. Thrown back again by the volume of fire, the Canadian militia broke contact and withdrew. Some Americans pursued but came into view of Canadians on the left bank, who opened fire across the water and checked their advance.

Stymied on both flanks and disheartened at the obvious lack of confidence shown in his force by the Secretary of War, Hampton ordered a general withdrawal. His division had lost about fifty men. Later, Wilkinson ordered him to continue on toward Montreal, but he refused, citing a lack of supplies and sickness among the troops. Hampton wrote to Armstrong:

> The force is dropping off by fatigue and sickness to a most alarming extent and, what is more discouraging, the officers, with a few exceptions, are sunk as low as the soldiers, and endure hardship and privation as badly. … Fatigue and suffering from the weather have deprived them of that spirit which constituted my best hopes.

Many of Hampton's officers were disgusted at their commander's lack of resolution in pressing the attack. Maj. John Ellis Wool, a particularly audacious and competent leader, later wrote of the battle that "no officer who had any regard for his own reputation, would voluntarily acknowledge himself as being engaged in it." One prong of the American offensive had been defeated, by stalwart Canadians to be sure, but also by confusion and mistrust in the mind of the commander, induced not by enemy action but by the intrigue and incompetence of superiors. Hampton would resign in March of the following year. When General Hampton was just starting his campaign, Wilkinson ordered his division of seven thousand soldiers to concentrate on Grenadier Island, halfway between Sackett's Harbor and Kingston. Wilkinson's quartermasters gathered large numbers of rivercraft to support the invasion. Then, Wilkinson changed his mind and opted to move against Montreal rather than Kingston. Chauncey protested. There were rapids along the river, complicating and slowing down movement. British batteries on shore could bring the American vessels under fire. It was late in the season and ice would hamper movement if the Americans did not take their objectives quickly. Also, Chauncey noted, his gunboats would be of less use supporting an assault on Montreal than a landing against Kingston. His protests fell on deaf ears.

▲ A 1796 profile portrait of Alexander Macomb, who would distinguish himself during the War of 1812 and would later take the elevated position of Commanding General of the United States Army. (National Portrait Gallery, Smithsonian Institution; gift of Mr. and Mrs. Paul Mellon)

Wilkinson organized his division into four brigades commanded by Brig. Gens. John Boyd, Jacob Brown, Leonard Covington, and Robert Swartout, and a reserve commanded by Col. Alexander Macomb. Wilkinson's division got underway on October 16 heading down the St. Lawrence in a convoy of schooners, bateaux, scows, and gunboats. When the British realized that Montreal, and not Kingston, was the object of the advance, the commander in Kingston sent out a brigade under Lt. Col. Joseph Morrison and a handful of rivercraft led by Cdr. William Mulcaster to shadow the Americans.

The American flotilla threaded its way through the picturesque Thousand Islands with Brown's and Macomb's brigades in the lead. Brown outranked Macomb and commanded the combined force. On November 1, Brown ordered his boats into a wide cove on the New York shore where French Creek entered the larger river. He pushed his boats up French Creek and placed two 18-pounder guns to cover his camp on a low bluff above the cove. Late in the afternoon, Commander Mulcaster caught up with Brown. Mulcaster led eight watercraft—schooners, sloops, and gunboats—but only three vessels could enter the cove due to wind and current. The Royal Navy officer wanted to destroy Brown's bateaux. Mulcaster's shipboard cannon and Brown's two guns exchanged fire for an hour. Unable to silence the American cannon, Mulcaster drew off. However, early the next morning the British squadron reappeared and this time the Americans were ready for them. During the night, Brown had his men build a furnace to heat the cannon balls red hot. The firefight was short. After the American guns set one gunboat ablaze, Mulcaster drew his force off. He feared that he would be trapped in the cove as the rest of the American vessels drew nearer. The British put out the fire and Mulcaster escaped with light casualties. The next day, the rest of Wilkinson's division arrived at French Creek.

Meanwhile, back at Fort George, Winfield Scott was chafing for combat. In a questionable interpretation of his orders, Scott had departed the Niagara River on October 13 with a few companies of the 2d U.S. Artillery and raced to join Wilkinson. The anxious and ambitious Scott left his slow-moving artillery and rode on by himself, finding the Americans on November 6. Scott pleaded for a

command. Since Macomb now commanded the reserve brigade, Wilkinson put Scott in charge of the 3d U.S. Artillery, Macomb's regiment. That day, Wilkinson first learned of Hampton's fight on the Chateauguay River. Assuming that Hampton would continue the advance, Wilkinson wrote to Hampton, directing the other division commander to link up with his column near Montreal Island.

The St. Lawrence River narrowed where the hamlet of Prescott on the Canadian shore faced the village of Ogdensburg, New York. Near Prescott, the British had thrown up earthworks to protect a battery of seventeen guns. Later, this small fortification would be named Fort Wellington. However, on November 6 this

77

nameless battery presented the first serious challenge to the American advance. Wilkinson ordered his men off their boats. They would trudge along the New York shore at night while the crews rowed the watercraft past the British guns. Fortunately, a fog covered much of the river between Ogdensburg and Prescott. Nonetheless, the British opened a relentless fire on any boats that came into view. By dawn, more than a hundred American boats had safely passed Prescott and only one American had died in the fierce cannonade.

Over the next several days, Canadian militia swarmed the northern shores of the St. Lawrence, firing cannon and muskets whenever American vessels drew nearby. Brown led his and Macomb's brigades at the head of the lengthy American convoy, landing as necessary to drive off British defenders. Brown's advance guard brigades also included Benjamin Forsyth's battalion of riflemen and about two hundred fifty horsemen from the 1st and 2d Regiments of Light Dragoons. Brown's troops moved along the roads paralleling the river, clearing the way forward despite destroyed bridges and sporadic enemy musketry.

Wilkinson, by now quite feverish and taking doses of laudanum, landed his remaining three brigades near the farm of prominent businessman, John Crysler, not far from the Long Sault Rapids. Boat pilots and crews would navigate about eight miles of rapids, while the soldiers marched along the northern shore, now

▼ A heavy infantry cannon looks out over the waters of the St. Lawrence River at the site of the battle of Crysler's Farm. The wooden wedge (called the quoin) under the cascabel was used to adjust elevation. (Michael/ CC BY 2.0)

cleared in front by Brown, Macomb, Scott, and Forsyth. Unfortunately for the Americans, Morrison was close to the American rear.

Colonel Morrison commanded a mixed group of British regulars, Canadian regulars and militia, and a small body of Indian warriors, about twelve hundred in all. The evening of November 10 was stormy, leaving all the soldiery wet and cold on the following morning. Morrison's light troops skirmished with the Americans on farmer Crysler's plowed fields and in the woods farther east. Commanding from his bed aboard ship, Wilkinson ordered Boyd to take command of the three American brigades and to drive off Morrison if the British approached. Early in the afternoon, Morrison did just that. Boyd, commanding about twenty-two hundred infantry and a small number of dragoons, turned the army about and ordered General Swartout to counterattack. Boyd and Covington would support the attack. The battle of Crysler's Farm had begun.

The Americans pushed a few companies of Canadian light troops westward through the woods for about a mile. During this movement, the American battalions became separated and disordered. Emerging from the wood line, the Americans saw British regulars drawn up for battle and came under fire from three 6-pounder cannon. The British guns fired spherical case shot, a hollow iron ball filled with twenty seven musket balls and gunpowder, fused to explode over the heads of troops. The U.S. artillery was still loaded on boats when the fighting began, and it took nearly two hours before four American 6-pounder guns entered the fray. Many American infantry, anxious to fight, fired their muskets without orders and sergeants struggled to restore order.

▶ A panoramic depiction of the battle of Crysler's Farm by artist Sheriff Scott. The image shows the serried ranks of the Anglo-Canadian force holding good order, while the American forces begin their collapse into disorder and retreat. (Lighbulbz/ CC BY-SA 4.0)

Boyd decided to attack the left flank of the British line. He ordered Swartout to use the woods north of the open fields for cover until he could attack directly into the British line. He sent his own brigade, under Col. Isaac Coles, to support Swartout. Canadian light troops and Mohawk warriors fired upon the American columns as

they struggled over fallen trees. As two U.S. battalions emerged from the woods and attempted to change formation from column into line, anxious American soldiers again opened fire despite the shouted commands of their leaders. The British initiated a controlled fire, which played havoc on the Americans struggling to overcome their disorder. Swartout's troops balked and slowly the battalions disintegrated, the men streaming back the way they had come. About the same time, Coles' men emerged from the woods, experienced the same heavy fire, and followed the example of Swartout's men.

General Covington, seeing the disorder on the right flank, formed his brigade into line and advanced directly on the British center. His men descended into a deep, water-filled ravine, crossed it with difficulty, and emerged onto a muddy field. British infantry and artillery opened fire immediately. Covington was mortally wounded in the opening volley, and he turned command of the brigade over to Col. Cromwell Pearce. Pearce got the brigade into enough order to continue the attack. Both sides engaged in a firefight. British musketry, the result of superb training, more than made up for inferior numbers. American companies and battalions lost cohesion, as the men sought cover where they could.

American artillery crews moved their four guns with great difficulty across the ravine and emerged about four hundred yards from the British line. The artillery did not have case shot, but fired canister instead. A canister round was essentially

◄ A granite obelisk is the most poignant marker at the Battle of Crysler's Farm National Historic Site of Canada, in Morrisburg, Ontario. Most of the original Crysler's Farm battle site, however, lies underwater. (Dennis G. Jarvis/CC BY-SA 2.0)

a tin can filled with musket balls and, like a shotgun blast, was devastating at close range. This deadly fire stabilized the battle somewhat as Swartout, Coles, and Pearce tried desperately to rally their men. Many of the infantrymen had exhausted their ammunition and the supply wagons were still on the boats. The British sent a battalion to capture the American guns, but the artillery easily repulsed this attack. American dragoons attacked the right of the British line but were themselves thrown back. Boyd, believing that he had carried out his orders to prevent the British from interfering with the advance downriver, ordered his brigades to withdraw and re-form. This left the British in possession of the battlefield and established their claim to the victory.

Wilkinson ordered the army to embark and to cross over to the American shore. Many officers and men complained that they had won the battle and could finish off the British the next day. They criticized Boyd's lack of determination and general incompetence.

He had committed battalions piecemeal allowing the enemy to defeat them individually. Lt. Joseph Hawley Dwight wrote in his journal: "To describe the battle correctly is impossible. There was no order or system displayed on our part. Our troops fought well when not disheartened by conflicting orders." Some, however, understood that the Americans would have to match their opponent's discipline and skill if they were to prevail.

The day after the battle, Wilkinson received a letter from Hampton revealing that he was returning to Plattsburgh. Wilkinson convened a council of war that reluctantly agreed that to pursue the campaign without Hampton's active support would be futile. He withdrew the army to winter quarters at French Mills, just inside the New York border.

The winter at Valley Forge, Pennsylvania, is etched into American memory. The more brutal conditions at French Mills in northern New York are largely forgotten. The men lived in tents while they built their huts. The quartermasters could not establish regular deliveries of food until late in December. On November 16, Lt. Reynold Kirby of the 3d U.S. Artillery recorded, "The face of the country where we are now located with a prospect of remaining a long time is wild & uninhabited—it will be long ere we shall be under the cover of our huts which we are about to erect. The weather is cold & the ice is forming in the river." Men starved, fell ill, and died. Wilkinson established a comfortable headquarters in the village of Four Corners, and he put Brown in charge of the division at French Mills. Wilkinson allowed many of his officers to depart the army to spend the winter at their homes. Finally, on Christmas Day, the men occupied their crude huts. Spring would bring new leaders and a new campaign.

Destruction on the Niagara, December 1813

When Wilkinson gathered his forces for the move on Montreal, he stripped Fort George of regulars. Militia Brig. Gen. George McClure took command of the post that had been in American hands since May. McClure's aide, Lt. William Rochester, wrote to his father: "The regulars here have all gone. We have about 800 militia here, who are completely raw, untrained, and lawless."

These militiamen, it seems, spent their days looting local Canadian farms. In early December, their short enlistments up, hundreds of militiamen returned to New York despite McClure's entreaties to remain at Fort George. With fewer than two hundred men, McClure could not maintain America's last toehold on the Niagara frontier. He decided to destroy the post and to return to the American side of the river. He also decided to burn the unoffending village of Newark, ostensibly to prevent British forces from using its homes as shelter.

Colonel Chapin of Buffalo, a medical doctor and the leader of a detachment of New York volunteers, argued forcibly that destroying the town would only invite retaliation. His arguments fell on deaf ears In the swirling snows of December 10, 1813, McClure's men ordered the citizens of Newark out of their homes and then torched the buildings. Nearly four hundred women, children, and elderly men, with little more than the clothes on their backs, sought shelter in the nearby farms. McClure's contingent then moved to Fort George and destroyed the main magazine and spiked some of the guns. However, they left the fort's wooden palisades intact as they returned to New York. The citizens on the American side of the border were aghast at the needless destruction and braced themselves for the reprisals sure to follow.

▼ The alliance forged between the British and many Native American tribes was regarded as the encouragement of savagery by American propagandists. Here the artist depicts Indians scalping American dead for British financial reward. (Missouri History Museum)

Arise, Columbia's Sons and forward press,
Your Country's wrongs, call loudly for redress,
The savage Indian with his scalping knife
Or tomahawk may seek to take your life,

MANE BRITISH AND THEIR WORTHY ALLIES!
Bring me the Scalps
and the King our Master
will reward you!
By bravery aw'd they'll in a dreadfull fright
Shrink back for refuge to the woods in flight,
Their British leaders then will quickly shake,
And for these wrongs shall restitution make.

Profile:
Bayonets

By the War of 1812, the bayonet was the chief auxiliary weapon of the infantryman. It had evolved from the early muzzle-plug types to the socket bayonet, which fitted around the muzzle of a musket via an open-tube socket, from which the bayonet projected to the side and forward, beneath the weapon's axis of fire. This configuration meant that the soldier could still fire his musket with the bayonet fitted, although the extra weight out front was to the detriment of accuracy, thus this tactic was unpopular. The rationale of the bayonet was as a close-quarters assault weapon. The theory went that the massed ranks of infantry would first engage the enemy with volley fire, then fix bayonets and launch a coordinated charge to overwhelm the enemy psychologically and physically. Such an approach worked well on flat European battlefields, but the fighting in North America made it more problematic. Complicated woodland terrain dispersed the charging ranks and more open skirmishing formations were unsuitable for a dense bayonet charge. U.S. troops also found that if hand-to-hand fighting was joined, knives and hatchets could be wielded with greater effect. Thus many bayonets were consigned to utility purposes, such as tent pegs or candle holders.

▲ Socket bayonets here provide a convenient way to store muskets at a War of 1812 re-enactment camp. For lengthier storage, soldiers would often plug the muzzle with a tampon, the touch-hole with a feather, and cover the flintlock mechanism with a special leather cover known as a "calf's knee." (The latter could also be used to keep powder dry on wet days.) (Corvair Owner/CC BY 2.0)

Follow they did. Late in the evening of December 18, a force of five hundred sixty British regulars crossed the Niagara River near Youngstown, a small settlement south of Fort Niagara. Approximately four hundred American regulars defended the fort, led by Capt. Nathan Leonard. Despite warnings of an impending raid, Leonard was not in the fortress, but rather at his home two miles away. The British commander in Upper Canada, Lt. Gen. Gordon Drummond, ordered his men to conduct a bayonet assault. Three parties of attackers, equipped with axes, scaling ladders, and unloaded muskets headed for the earthen bastions and the main gate. Entry into the fort was effortless; the American sentries had left the main gate unlocked to ease the passage of guards.

Swarming into Fort Niagara, British infantry quickly subdued most of the garrison. The stoutest resistance came from the sick in the hospital. In obedience to General Drummond's intent, the British went about their grisly work, even killing Americans as they surrendered. When dawn arrived, sixty-five Americans and six British were dead. The British would hold Fort Niagara until the end of the war.

British Maj. Gen. Phineas Riall followed up the capture of the fort with a devastating early morning raid on the American shore. A force of one thousand British soldiers and five hundred allied Indians attacked the villages of Lewiston, Manchester (now Niagara Falls), and the Tuscarora Indian village. Taken by surprise, the militia put up a feeble resistance. Soon hundreds of civilians were fleeing eastward. The native warriors took scalps freely until stopped by British officers. The soldiers torched every structure along the river.

Jonas Harrison, the collector of customs for the District of Niagara, wrote to his superior:

> The citizens about Lewiston and its vicinity below the slope or highland that forms the Falls of Niagara escaped by the Ridge Road towards Genesee Falls, all going the one road, on foot, old and young, men, women, and children, flying from their beds, some not more than half dressed without shoes or stockings, together with men on horseback, wagons, carts, sleighs and sleds, overturning and crushing each other, stimulated by the horrid yells of the 900 savages on the pursuit, which lasted eight miles, formed a scene awful and terrific in the extreme. The small military force we had were the first to fly.

Riall followed up this foray with a raid on the villages of Black Rock and Buffalo. In the early hours of December 30, one thousand British regulars and four hundred Indian warriors crossed the Niagara River north of Black Rock. The Americans were more prepared this time. They had hounded the deplorable McClure out of command. His replacement, Maj. Gen. Amos Hall, gathered about two thousand militiamen from the local counties. The Americans offered a stronger resistance, but the fear of British bayonets and Indian scalping knives was palpable. By the end of the day, thirty-one British and about an equal number of Americans lay dead. The British took one hundred thirty prisoners; the rest of the militiamen escaped to their homes. The civilians were not so fortunate; hundreds fled in the snow, seeking shelter to the east. Riall, according to plan, torched nearly every structure within his reach. Twelve days later, General Cass wrote to Secretary of War Armstrong: "I passed this day the ruins of Buffalo. It exhibits a scene of distress and destruction such as I have never before witnessed."

Analysis

Despite marked improvements in the Regular Army during 1813, strategic success eluded the American cause. Mediocre leaders made too many faulty operational decisions and failed to press the fight despite opposition. Harrison's and Perry's triumphs in the west did not translate into success elsewhere. The war along the border with Canada would continue into 1814.

President Madison and Secretary of War Armstrong rightly understood that the capture of either Montreal or Quebec would cut the British line of communications and result in the strangulation of all resistance to the west. Nonetheless, Washington directed that the major efforts of 1813 were to reestablish American control over the Northwest and to defeat the British on Lake Ontario. Dearborn and Chauncey compounded this strategic misdirection when they expended their efforts against York and Fort George instead of Kingston, the center of gravity of British operations in Upper Canada. Chauncey believed that the capture of the naval stores and armament at York would irrevocably shift the balance of naval power to his Lake Ontario squadron. Despite the American victory at York, the shift proved limited at best. The Americans captured food and equipment destined for British forces to the west, contributing to Harrison's victory in western Upper Canada. However, the loss of Pike, a competent and inspiring leader, was tragic.

▼ The War of 1812 monument on Parliament Hill, Ottawa, entitled "Triumph Through Diversity," depicts seven figures: a Métis fighter operating a cannon; a woman bandaging the arm of a Voltigeur; a Royal Navy sailor; a First Nations warrior; a Canadian militiaman, and a member of the Royal Newfoundland Regiment. (Jeangagnon/CC BY-SA 4.0)

Likewise, the capture of Fort George had led to a very limited improvement in the American situation. Once the Americans had seized the fort, they had to retain it. The defense of Fort George, and the appalling losses at Stoney Creek and Beaver Dams, bled the American army of valuable manpower. In the end, the British pinned down an American division until Armstrong and Wilkinson shifted the focus of American action against Montreal, where it should have been in the first place. Armstrong acted weakly in dealing with his subordinates and lost valuable time in choosing the objective of the operation. He could not quell the feud between Wilkinson and Hampton, and their lack of trust doomed the campaign from the beginning.

1812 - 1

Some blame for the disappointing failures of 1813 must rest at the feet of the national government, which failed to mobilize the country's resources. Congress and the Madison administration had not entirely understood the difficulties of expanding the army and navy from their meager prewar strengths. Few citizens were willing to join the Regular Army despite increases in pay and shortening of enlistment terms. There were not enough experienced officers and non-commissioned officers to train the many new regular and volunteer regiments. Dependence on state militias was misplaced. Acquiring supplies and food and moving these commodities to the frontiers of America were daunting tasks never satisfactorily accomplished. While soldiers were adequately armed, they often lacked warm clothing and frequently went hungry.

Perhaps the gravest mistake the administration made was in its choice of generals. Of the four men Madison had promoted to major general, only Harrison pressed the fight. Wilkinson, Hampton, and Lewis were all disappointments. Among the brigadier generals, Boyd, Chandler, and Winder all exhibited personal courage yet performed inadequately. Fortunately, the year's events had allowed the President to identify a few competent officers, such as Brown, Macomb, and Scott, whom he could turn to in the coming year. It remained to be seen whether these men could build upon the trials and disappointments of the previous eighteen months to forge a more effective army.

Further Reading

Elliott, James E. Strange Fatality: *The Battle of Stoney Creek, 1813.* Toronto: Robin Brass Studio, 2009.

Everest, Allan S. *The War of 1812 in the Champlain Valley.* Syracuse, N.Y.: Syracuse University Press, 1981.

Gilpin, Alec R. *The War of 1812 in the Old Northwest.* East Lansing: Michigan State University Press, 1958.

Graves, Donald E. *Field of Glory: The Battle of Crysler's Farm, 1813.* Toronto: Robin Brass Studio, 1999.

Hickey, Donald R. *The War of 1812: A Forgotten Conflict.* Urbana: University of Illinois Press, 1989.

Mahon, John K. *The War of 1812.* Gainesville: University of Florida Press, 1972.

Malcomson, Robert. *Capital in Flames: The American Attack on York, 1813.* Toronto: Robin Brass Studio, 2008.

Malcomson, Robert. *Lords of the Lake: The Naval War on Lake Ontario, 1812–1814.* Annapolis, Md.: Naval Institute Press, 1998.

Skaggs, David Curtis and Gerard T. Altoff. *A Signal Victory: The Lake Erie Campaign, 1812–1813.* Annapolis, Md.: Naval Institute Press, 1997.

Wilder, Patrick A. *The Battle of Sackett's Harbour: 1813.* Baltimore, Md.: Nautical and Aviation Publishing Company of America, 1994.

Index